T0078103

DIARY OF AN IRISH GRANDMA

D E D I C A T E D   T O   M Y   G I R L S

KATHY KELLY

authorHOUSE®

AuthorHouse™
1663 Liberty Drive
Bloomington, IN 47403
www.authorhouse.com
Phone: 833-262-8899

© 2020 Kathy Kelly. All rights reserved.

No part of this book may be reproduced, stored in a retrieval system, or
transmitted by any means without the written permission of the author.

Published by AuthorHouse 08/31/2020

ISBN: 978-1-7283-7126-9 (sc)
ISBN: 978-1-7283-7237-2 (e)

Print information available on the last page.

Any people depicted in stock imagery provided by Getty Images are models,
and such images are being used for illustrative purposes only.
Certain stock imagery © Getty Images.

This book is printed on acid-free paper.

Because of the dynamic nature of the Internet, any web addresses or links contained in
this book may have changed since publication and may no longer be valid. The views
expressed in this work are solely those of the author and do not necessarily reflect the
views of the publisher, and the publisher hereby disclaims any responsibility for them.

GROWING UP IN IRELAND

The date was April 15, 1946, the place was a town in the Irish Republic called Carrickmacross, Co. Monaghan. The event was my birthday. The time in history was the end of WW11, the start of the baby boom although you will see from my family history the baby boom was well on it's way. Big families was the norm in Ireland. Hello! My name at birth was Olivia Katherine Ann Clarke. It was the custom to call the first boy after the grandfathers and likewise the first girl after the grandmothers so that's where the Katherine Ann came from, Olivia was after my mother's favorite movie star Olivia de Havilland who died this week at 104. I was number two in a family that later grew to nine in a matter of 11 years. My mother, Peggy (Margaret) Allen was one of 12 and most of them lived on our street including my grandmother. My father, Mick (Michael) Clarke was one of 12 who came from Crossmaglen, Co. Armagh in Northern Ireland. We had two towns wrapped up. The only bad thing about that was that we could do nothing on the sly there were too many eyes on us. I will be making reference to my siblings from time to time so here are their names in chronological order: Tom, Olive, Irene, Patricia (RIP), Mary, Thecla, Michael (RIP), Gerard and Regina.

A little geography lesson here: Ireland is broken up into 32 countries, 6 of which are in the north under British rule. The south is referred to as the Republic or the Free State.

My Granda Allen, died at 49 of cancer. They had a lodging house and restaurant across the street from us so we never went hungry. My Granda Clarke also died at 49 from cancer. They had a grocery store on the square in Crossmaglen. My father was a horse dealer so we grew

1

up with horses, cows, pigs, goats, chickens, you name it we had it even though we lived in the town. We had 4 fields out the Dundalk Road. There were always people in our house mostly horse dealers and my mother's family were in and out all the time. I don't remember much about my early years except a slew of babies one after another. Actually my sister Irene and I are Irish twins, just 10 months apart. As an older sister it was my job to take the babies for a walk every day, one baby lying down in the pram (carriage), another one sitting at the bottom of it, one walking on each side holding on to the handles. My sister had just as many of my aunt's kids as we walked out to the end of the foot path on the Dundalk road. There was always a pram outside our front door with a baby in it and our dog Spot lay underneath keeping guard, nobody could get anywhere close to it. With all those kids I never remember feeding one or changing a diaper, just walking them so I didn't have it that bad, it could have been a lot worse.

Not Another Baby

We ran back-and-forth to granny's restaurant especially if we didn't like what mammy was cooking. I remember a lady who worked for granny and whenever she came to our house and started cleaning and hanging up baby clothes over the fire, that was the signal we were going to have another baby. You could barely tell when a mother was pregnant because they hid it under a big wrap around apron not like nowadays, they show off their belly. They didn't even talk about it in front of kids. They'd say "so and so is exp." I guess they forgot we learned to spell in school. I remember one morning lying in bed, I was ten years old and I heard my mother screaming or laughing or crying I couldn't tell, thought maybe daddy was telling her jokes. Then daddy flying down the stairs taking two steps at a time. Back he came with the mid wife who he found in the church, and then came the dreaded baby cry. I was also crying because I thought not another baby to take for walks but I guess they didn't have to ask for my permission. That turned out to be my sister Regina, number nine. You'd think I'd know the signals after all those kids.

It seemed there was never a time when there wasn't a baby in our house. We only had two bedrooms, actually three but one was damp and cold so daddy stored horse's harness in it. By the time our family was complete the ten of us slept in two bedrooms. There were at least two cribs in mammy and daddy's room and three kids in a bed there, then in the other bedroom we had two full-size beds where Tom, Irene and I slept. Bedtime for us meant dressing up in the bed sheets and having concerts. One time we heard the neighbors clap underneath our window because they were listening to us sing. We were very musical, got up singing to the radio in the morning and went to bed singing with a few fights in between, we loved music. We didn't have birthday parties and we had to keep track of our own birthday, usually someone reminded us. I have that problem today but there's a good excuse, it's called senility. Mary and Irene had their birthdays reversed.

Breakfast In Bed

When I was nine years old I started getting up first in the morning, and I lit the fire with newspapers, sticks and coal and waited for it to get hot. I'd boil the kettle and bring tea and toast up to everyone because they wouldn't get up until they got their breakfast in bed. Toast was a pain in the butt because I had to put a fork into each slice, hold it up to this little slot in the front of the range and then turn it to toast the other side. I had to do this ten times, one slice for each of us. One morning I was raking the fire when I found a roll of white notes tied with a rubber band in the ashes. It was money, Daddy must have accidentally dropped it in the fire. Just one spark and it would have gone up in smoke. I remember when we got our first Kosangas stove. Mammy got me out of bed to show me how to use it so now I didn't have to light a fire to boil the kettle and there was even a grill on top where I could toast 2 slices of bread at a time. Boy, was I a happy camper, I could get breakfast in half the time now. I just saw a commercial for air fryers that can toast 6 slices at a time wow! Everyone took 2 spoons of sugar and milk with their tea so that made it easy. I took it that way for years until one day at work I couldn't leave my desk to get either sugar or milk and I took it straight and I've been taking it that way ever since. We can be such creatures of habit. Since we ate dinner at noon we'd have a banana or tomato sandwich in the evening and corn flakes or porridge with hot milk at night. Friday was fish day, mostly herrings. Daddy usually cleaned them but one day he was away and I did it. I'd seen him do it several times. But I wouldn't clean out a chicken or a turkey for a pension.

Mammy was very particular about manners, we had to be excused before leaving the table and always answered pardon never what. We ate with a knife and fork, no using our fingers and sat like a lady with our dress down over our knees. We were polite in company, thank you, please, excuse me etc. and never interrupted adults. Above all respect our elders. We greeted people on the street with a smile and a hello, sometimes "how are ya". My mother would say how do you spell that. She was a great speller and always quizzing us. One time we were down the town and I saw a truck with "demesne" written on it and mammy turned to me and said how do you spell demesne and I was ready for her.

Saturday night was bath night. A big aluminum bath tub was supported on two chairs in our kitchen and we had to boil kettles of water. One by one we climbed into the tub, youngest to oldest. Anyone could have walked in on us our front door was always open. One time our little budgie flew into it and drowned. As we got older we went over to Grannys for our bath. Electricity to heat the water was expensive so we were only allowed to fill the tub up once. By the time the last ones got in the water was cold and dirty. We didn't have hot running water in our house so we carried buckets of hot water from Grannys on laundry day. Today they use cold water, go figure! Mammy had a washing machine with a hand wringer, then the clothes were hung out on clothes lines in granny's back yard because we had animals in ours. When the sun went down or it started to rain we took them in to finish drying on a line with a pulley from the kitchen ceiling or on a railing over the fire. Some things had to be rewashed because birds would crap on them. Then came the ironing, they ironed sheets, pillowcases, handkerchiefs, underwear and socks. Even as a kid I thought that was ridiculous. I could see some things because we didn't have permanent press but not that kind of stuff. One time I accidently put a pillowcase in with daddy's hankies and when he shook it out a mass he was embarrassed. We wore uniforms to school and we changed our underwear and socks Sunday and Wednesday. The socks were turned inside out between changes. Mammy used Tide and a washboard to scrub our white socks and the boy's shirt collars until her poor knuckles bled.

The Dreaded School Days

We were lucky we didn't have too far to walk to school not like the poor country kids. They had to ride their bikes or walk miles, hail, rain or snow after doing a day's work on the farm and sit there all day in wet clothes. No school buses then. They usually carried a bottle of milk and two slices of buttered bread for their lunch and had their dinner in the evenings. We were close enough we could run home for dinner at noon time. When we arrived at school we put dusters under our feet and polished the hardwood floors before we started class. Everyone made their own dusters. We had a nun who inspected our fingernails and she slapped us with the cane if they weren't clean. She was a little bit of a thing but boy she could hit hard. One time she hit a kid so hard the kid fell backwards against the blackboard and it fell on top of her. My father called them frustrated old maids.

Some of our clothes were hand me downs, they were sometimes faded and as the oldest girl that didn't mean I got new ones, my uniform was handed down from the neighbors and went from me to my sisters. We started school at 4 or earlier if you were close to the cutoff date so some kids were only 3. There were such big families then I guess the mothers were glad to get the kids out of the house. We had babies and high infants classes, that would be the equivalent to pre-k and kindergarten. One time I was called out of babies class, my aunt was at the door with my knickers in her pocket. I had forgotten to put them on that morning. We wore navy blue knickers practically down to our knees, it's a wonder I didn't feel the draught. My sister reminded me she had a similar experience. Every Friday there was a penny collection for the black babies and once a year each family had to pay coal money to keep the school heated. We knew this guy who said he got held back so many times in first grade he was shaving. The kids thought he was the teacher.

I remember in first grade we were learning to knit and one of my needles must have fallen out of my homemade cloth knitting bag which was easy because they had a point at both ends. I had to line up with the rest for a slap. The nun used these big thick pointers and she broke it on a kids hand ahead of me so we all turned around and went back to our seats. She opened the cabinet and here it was stacked high with pointers, so now she had a fresh new one which was harder than the old. Also in first grade my mother was teaching me my catechism the night before and there was the word excommunication in the answer and I couldn't pronounce it. It was too big, I was only six years old and the next day the nun asked me the question and I couldn't get past the word so she whacked me. I went home for lunch crying and told my mother. She told our neighbor's daughter who was 2 years older to tell the nun if she ever slapped me again she was going to take me out of there and send me to Protestant school, like that was ever going to happen, it was unheard of for a catholic kid to go to Protestant school. Catholics were afraid God would strike them dead if they entered a Protestant church or grave yard. One time we sneaked into a Protestant graveyard, it was very creepy, almost haunted and one of the head stones read "he is not dead but sleeping". We were out of there like a bullet in case he woke up. Besides that we believed only Catholics went to Heaven. I remember thinking when I grew up I was going to try and convert all the Protestants so they could go to Heaven too. I knew that would be a big undertaking but I was going to try. We also had the fear of being struck dead if we told a lie, that's why we don't make good politicians, on second thought strike that. I blushed an awful lot so lying was out for me, my face would give me away. I even blushed when I was innocent so that made me look guilty. Boy wouldn't I like to blush today through my wrinkled old pale skin.

Working In Grannys

We got home for dinner at noon every day but we had to run fast because we only had 40 minutes. We tried to hide from the old ladies standing at their doors waiting to catch us to go to the shop for cigarettes. We would gulp down our dinner and then run over to grannys to wait on tables or wash dishes. There were two factories in town, the shoe factory and the jam factory. A lot of the workers came to grannys for dinner. The bottom dining room was for the women, the top for the men, the middle one for all other plus the lodgers. I liked to serve in the top room because it was all men and they were easy to please, the women were too fussy. Every other word out of the men's mouths was F.... this, F....that, they couldn't say two words without it. There was no menu, everyone got the same thing, soup, meat, potatoes, vegetables and a cookie or a slice of buttered bread with tea after dinner. I went back to school with grease marks on my arms from washing dishes. In those days there was no dishwashing liquid so you just used plain hot water.

Granny was very thrifty, I guess she had to be. Her husband was dead and she had a family of 12 to support although some were grown and working in the shoe factory. I remember one time the cat grabbed a piece of steak and ran down the yard with it. My aunt chased after the cat, got the meat, rinsed it off and put it on the pan. I never heard of anyone getting sick from there so I guess it was ok. The show bands ate there before a dance, we loved serving them because they'd recognize us at the dance and wave to us from the stage. Granny had a second toilet down the back yard next to the pigsty. My aunt said one time a rat jumped up and bit her while she was going. Needless to say nobody was in any hurry to use it.

The "Luxuries" Of Home

Let's get back to our house. We didn't have a bathroom or hot water, just an outside toilet. Once again we had the fear of mice or rats jumping up at us because of all the animals and hay and there was no outside light. Daddy cut up the Sunday newspaper and hung it on a nail with a piece of twine, there was no such thing as toilet paper, some people used leaves. I don't know if that contributed to hemorrhoids in later life or wearing the latest news on our butt. Chilblains was another problem. Because of the cold we hatched the fire to get warm and burned our shins and feet. There were a few cures for that, ie run barefoot in the snow or put your feet in a pee pot. I tried both with no success. The cure was to stay away from the fire. The stove only heated the kitchen, the rest of the house was damp and cold. The dampness ran down the walls upstairs. We had a small electric heater in our bedroom where we'd warm our pajamas. We sat around it playing with movie star cards that came with bubble gum or paper dressing dolls. I was Olivia de Havilland after my names sake, my sister was Elizabeth Taylor. Boys got sports figures.

We had one wardrobe in our bed room (now we have walk in closets) and our clothes were wet with dampness coming out of it. Our mattresses were made of horsehair so we often had fleas. Out came the DDT, we slept on the bed right after it was sprayed. It was sprayed directly on the dog if we saw him scratching. It wasn't unusual to see kids scratching flea bites on their legs at school. Mammy cleaned upstairs every Saturday morning while we were still in bed. It was the only morning we got to sleep late. She'd threaten to throw our clothes under the bed if we didn't hang them up, same story every Saturday. We didn't have that much clothes to make a mess. It was my job to clean the new stove every Saturday, I treated that like gold. We washed the dishes in a basin on the kitchen table after boiling a kettle of water. And no drip dry, we needed them for the next meal, there were 10 of us. Like all good respectable Irish people we polished the front door brass knob and knocker every Saturday.

Our house was never empty, cousins, neighbors and horse dealers visited during the day and mammy's family at night. My mother dreaded a rainy weekend because we couldn't go outside. Our cousins lived down the street but spent most of their time in our house. One was chubby and he cleaned off the leftovers on our plates. Then there was the little thief who used to steal Gerard's toy soldiers and cowboys and Indians.

On his way out the door Gerard would say "get over here 'til I search you". Sure enough he always had something in his pockets. My mother bought a cane once and hung it at the bottom of the stairs. Every time she reached for it it was gone. Mary was upstairs playing school dressed as a nun whacking the bed (the kids). A neighbor friend was upstairs playing school one day and when she tried to leave our front door was locked so she opened the bedroom window and jumped out. We thought she'd break something but she didn't. No one ever tried that again. On nice days we played house in our gateway, no toys, just a broom to make walls out of the dust and our imagination.

At about 9 years old I learned to bake from auntie Phyllis, never a recipe, just a handful of this and a wee drop a that. Every Sunday afternoon I baked a Kerry apple pie and a sponge cake. It seemed they were no sooner out of the oven when a car would pull up in front of our house loaded down with daddy's relatives. I say loaded down because some of daddy's sisters were overweight, they were diabetic. Granny used to say "here's me head, the rest of me's comin". That was the end of my cakes, they were gone in one round with a cup of tea. The men went to the pub while the women sat around talking and God forbid we interrupt them, we were told children should be seen and not heard.

My Siblings

My sister Mary was a real crier, every morning she cried before she went to school. Something was always wrong with the turn up on her sleeves or the turn down on her socks, always something to cry about. Mammy would put her out in the backyard to shut her up and the neighbor would bring her back in. She claims she was an unhappy child because our little sister Patricia died of pneumonia a month before she was born and mammy was probably in mourning for the first few months of her life. She could be right, I'll give her the benefit of the doubt. She was the only one who got styes on her eyes, we figured it was from crying. Daddy it seems had the cure, a fasting spit, it was probably laced with stout from the night before. She even got to stay up later than the rest at night, that's how she got nick named "the fairy". I thought it was because she was the pet but I later learned that mammy was keeping her up late because she wet the bed. I have one more tale to tell about her: from the time shoulder pads became popular she wore them in everything, she even sewed them into her nightgowns when she went to the hospital. As an adult she's just like mammy, very particular about her appearance. She's working from home because of Covid-19 and she gets dressed up, makeup and all just to work at home. Others welcome the chance to work in their PJs.

I'm not going to let my youngest brother Gerard off the hook. He was tight as tuppance (2 pennies). We took turns buying biscuits for our tea after dinner. Usually we had to buy a half pound so each could get at least one. When it was his turn he'd buy a quarter pound of the cheapest, skinniest biscuits (Marietta) because they stretched further. He was always borrowing money from mammy, she said he had his first communion money. He was the comedian of the family, still is. Like me, he was blessed with donkey ears so when the beatle era came about he grew his hair and still keeps it long because it covers his ears. The next one of the family was Michael better known as the gangster of the family. Whenever anything went missing, he was the prime suspect especially if jewelry was involved. My sister discovered he was selling it to her boss' housekeeper probably for the price of a pack of cigarettes. He was that way right up to the end, always living on the edge.

Thecla was chubby and lazy as a young kid. She would sit in a chair and wait for someone to put her shoes and socks on and tie her laces before school. She ate everything in sight, one time we caught her sitting on the floor eating slops out of the pig's bucket. As a teenager she was a horse of a different color. She was way ahead of the rest of us, we knew very little about her extra curricular activities, she claims nobody cared. I guess the less we knew the better. She went out with teddy boys who wore drainpipes and had slicked back greasy hair. I don't remember her going to the dances much, she'd look into the Catholic hall before buying a ticket to see if there were any tall guys because she was the tallest of us girls. When she first got her period mammy asked me to show her how to use a sanitary napkin. I'm sure she knew as much as myself, maybe more. Being the oldest girl I was totally unprepared. I thought I was dying and I didn't want to tell my mother because I didn't want her to be sad about me bleeding to death. Finally I confided in an older cousin and she told me the facts of life and got me sanitary napkins and my first bra. Now I could straighten up instead of being hunched over hiding my new found boobs such as they were. I think I was behind the door when God was giving out boobs.

We had a milking cow, Daisy, but none of us liked fresh milk so we gave it to the neighbors that is if Michael didn't get to Daisy first and sell it. There was no such thing as canned or frozen vegetables, everything was fresh from the farm even if it was sprayed with DDT and milk was delivered daily in a glass bottle with the cream on the top and left on the window sill. Here we were giving away our cow's milk and buying pasteurized milk from the milkman. You could get bread in the local store but we loved the cottage loaves that the bread man sold from his van on Saturday nights but with the size of our family we were lucky to get two slices each out of a loaf. My aunt used to bake wheaten and soda bread. When we got home from school in the evenings we had a slice of bread with butter and jam and played outside until dark or until we got called in for the rosary.

Our Beloved Granny

Granny played a big role in our lives, she was always there for us. And she was the only one that could control daddy. Whenever he got drunk and out of hand someone would go get her. She would come to our house, didn't have to say a word just sit there and daddy wouldn't open his mouth. She had a way about her, I was afraid of her too although my sisters loved her. They sat in her living room by the fire reading library books, love stories no less. Granny wore a wrap around pinny (apron) and she'd pull it up in front and fill it with butter, potatoes, meat, eggs and rashers for us. My aunt did the same for our cousins. I don't know what we would've done without them. Granny never put a penny in the bank, she hid her money under her mattress. Whenever there was an auction in the town she'd be there cash in hand. She bought a business for her two unmarried daughters and gave all the rest cash while she was still alive.

My Bad Luck With Horses

I mentioned we kept horses and one time my father put me on one he had just bought to see how it rode. He told me to ride it down to the end of the street, turn around and come back, sounds simple enough right! Except when it was time to come back I couldn't get the horse to turn and so it went galloping out the road. Cars were beeping their horns because we were in the middle of the road, people were waving, I guess they thought I was just out for a ride. Finally I managed to turn the horse around. He came galloping back out of control, rode past daddy and took off down by the convent. If the horse didn't kill me I thought my father would. He chased after me in the car and as usual I was a useless good for nothing, the usual stuff, God forbid he ever paid us a compliment although when he died his drinking buddies said he was always bragging about us in the pub, that's nice! Another time when I was 16 he was giving me a leg up on a horse but the horse stepped back and stood on my foot. So here's daddy pushing me up with one foot and the horse standing on the other. It nearly crippled me and I was going to a dance that night. I could hardly walk let alone dance but wild horses couldn't keep me away.

Speaking of wild horses we had one wild horse nobody wanted to ride but there was this big bully who lived on the back lane. We invited him to ride the horse, he was delighted, he didn't know the horse bucked. True to form the horse started bucking as soon as he got up on him, we were all laughing at him and him f...n away, shame on us! Another time we went to a horse show and daddy put me on a horse and told me to jump it which I'd never done before. When the horse jumped he threw me over his head and I ended up with my arms around his neck looking into his face, I was close enough to kiss him. Daddy told me to get back up and hold onto the horse tight and not let him throw me. I did just that, I held on so tight that I banged my chin on his mane and had a big black chin for a week, least I didn't let him throw me. I guess I wasn't cut out to be a jockey.

My older brother Tom was the jockey of the family and was in charge of feeding the animals, cleaning out the stalls, milking the cow and walking the animals back and forth to the fields. He had to do it alone because the next 4 were girls. He won lots of prizes at horse shows. I remember one time daddy bought a piebald (palomino) pony that had his stomach ripped open on a barbed wire fence. Daddy stitched the horse up, made a sling and hung him from the ceiling of the stable and stayed up with him at night and nursed him back to good health. Who needs a veterinarian! Tom had this horse jumping through hoops in no time, they were made for each other. He also rode him at shows. One time someone was home from America and they bought the horse from daddy and believe it or not they wanted to take my brother too and train him to be a jockey. I didn't know you could sell the kid with the horse. I overheard mammy and daddy discussing whether they should let Tom go or not and I remember thinking oh my God they're actually considering giving my brother away. It wasn't a very secure feeling. Needless to say he didn't go to America but he did go to France. He had a pen pal when he was about 12 years old and she invited him over for a visit. He went and loved it and came home telling us all about the French people and how they drank wine with their supper, and carried long loaves of bread under their arm, all kinds of good stuff.

Daddy And The Gypsies

Daddy did a lot of business with the Gypsies. It wasn't unusual to come home and see gypsy kids eating at the kitchen table. The Gypsies sent their kids door to door begging for money but everyone knew if they gave them money the parents would use it for booze so people fed the kids and gave them clothes. Gypsies were known to be thieves, everything they sold fell off the back of a truck. Mammy bought linoleum from them for our kitchen and hallway. There was a lot of traffic coming through our house so she replaced it every year. Then she got down on her hands and knees and washed it every Saturday night. My aunt used to say "why don't you make one of those big girls do that for you". Mammy's response was "they'll be doing it long enough" and boy was she right! We had no problem helping but she wouldn't let us use the mop and we weren't getting down on our hands and knees when there was an easier way.

Getting back to the Gypsies, Daddy bought a caravan from them and we used to play in it up the back yard. It had this smokey smell, we would find lots of loose change buried between the cushions. Mary and her friend became very friendly with a Gypsy woman who was camped out the road. She taught them how to make flowers out of tissue paper, the men mended pots and pans. They were a bit mysterious but we were intrigued by them. Daddy "loaned" them money and they'd promise to pay him back when they got their children's allowance, a Government subsidy, but more often than not they were long gone by the 1st. of the month. My brother Gerard was much more shrewd than daddy, when he loaned them money he took their children's allowance books and they couldn't collect without him going with them. Everybody got this allowance, the more kids, the more money although I don't think that's what motivated the Irish to have big families. There was no birth control, the rhythm method was the word of the day but I don't think men cared about that when they had a few drinks. The Catholic teaching was "you have as many kids as God wills you to have". He must have loved the Irish. Gypsy kids didn't go to school but they were street wise. If the police came after the parents for not sending them to school they'd just move on to the next town. It was a sad way of life for the kids but least they weren't subjected to the wrath of the nuns and the brothers.

Our Daily Bread

Every Saturday night Daddy would leave 30 shillings ($5) on the mantle piece for mammy to buy the groceries. I think he thought it would last the week but it just bought the Sunday dinner. We had to pick pocket the rest when he was asleep. We didn't think we were stealing because it was for the house, better there than the pub. All the rest granny supplied because we all helped out in the restaurant.

Everyone thought daddy was the most decent man in the world and he was. He loaned them money because some of them bet the horses and were broke until payday. I loved my mother and father, I used to kneel down at night and pray that God would never let them get old. Be careful what you pray for because mammy died at forty nine and daddy seventy four.

In those days there were no refrigerators or freezers so we went to the butchers every day and I can still remember our order, a pound and a half of lean stewing meat and a few bones. The butchers was usually packed with everyone gossiping so I had to keep memorizing it in case I'd forget. I never remember us going hungry or wanting for anything. Mammy set a bowl of jelly (jello) every Saturday night for the Sunday dessert. We'd have half of it gone tasting it before it set. We usually had boiled chicken or pickled tongue on Sunday and it was gross watching my mother wrap that thing around in a pot of boiling water. I hated it, but it tasted a little better the next day when she sliced it and fried it on the pan but the very thought of eating a cow's tongue was gross. The only vegetable I ate was mushy peas so mammy always had some on the side of the stove for me. We had two tables in our kitchen, a small one by the window for the three boys and the rest sat at the big table. The boys would kick each other under the table and you'd hear f... off. Michael was usually the instigator. My mother was always worried there'd be a priest passing by our window and hear the cursing. There was a little press (cub board) under the window and at night we'd hear noise coming from it. They said it was mice but nobody was going near it to find out. We had another cub board going up the stairs which no one would reach into except Michael because he knew that's where mammy hid her wallet. I wouldn't have put my hand in there even if there was $100 bill sticking out for fear of mice or rats.

We picked mushrooms in the fields, none of us liked them because people used to say they were dog's farts. Daddy was the only one who ate them, he'd peel the outer skin off and put a dab of butter in the middle and cook them on the top of the stove. We also picked gooseberries and blackberries along the roadside but we ate them as fast as we picked them. Then there were the shamrocks growing along the railroad tracks. You had to wash them because they often smelled of animal's pee. My mother's birthday was St. Patrick's Day, she said the bands were out playing the day she was born. In case you don't know the significance of the shamrock, St. Patrick used it to convert the Irish pagans to Christianity, the three leaves of the shamrock represented the three persons in the Blessed Trinity, the Father, the Son and the Holy Spirit and it miraculously only grows around March 17th, the feast of St. Patrick, the patron saint of Ireland. And while we're on the subject, it was St. Patrick who drove the snakes out of Ireland and He asked God to spare the Irish the terrible events at the end of the world and it's said God promised him Ireland would drown three days before the end of the world. I always thought that's not fair, then everyone would have three days advance notice to get their souls in order. Every time I hear of a flood in Ireland I wonder is this it?

Our Choir Days

We had two old maids, and their brother, living next-door to us. They were caring for their handicapped sister and her two daughters. They weren't related but we called them aunt and uncle. They were highly respected because one had worked in the bank at one time and the family were cattle dealers. They played the organ in the church so whenever we'd see them pass by our kitchen window we'd run upstairs and hide. We'd tell Mammy to say we weren't home but she'd always call us down stairs and make us go with them to sing in the choir. They were afraid no one would show up to sing and there were times when we were the only ones there. God blessed us with a good voice and we should be happy to use it to sing for Him. I remember when their brother died the sisters were angry at God for taking away their sole support. They covered up all the holy pictures on the walls for a time but they finally came around. I thought he was old anyway but I later learned he was only fifty nine.

Granny had a Singer sewing machine with foot pedals and she taught me how to sew. She used to patch the boys pants. I loved to sew and I still do to this day. As I became a teenager I liked it even more because her sewing machine was in the kitchen in the new house where her lodgers watched TV and I had a crush on one though he never noticed me. Years later he dated my sister Mary. I remember the first time I wore lipstick my father looked at me and said what's the matter with your mouth, is it bleeding, get that stuff off you. I was humiliated because it was in front of yet another crush, who also didn't notice me. I stayed up 'til midnight the night I turned sixteen, the age of freedom but my mother reminded me every now and then it was twenty one. I was always full of gas (I later found out I was lactose intolerant) and whenever I let go Daddy would ask what's that smell then the poor dog got blamed and put outside in the cold. Better him than me.

We had our clothes made by a dressmaker because there were only two Protestant drapery stores in our town and they were very expensive. She also made my Irish dancing costume and a family friend embroidered it. The same person taught me to embroider serviettes. My dress was all Celtic signs, beautiful and an embroidered cape. I wore it all through primary school until I outgrew it. Mammy sold it for 30 shillings to an Englishman who was staying in Grannys. I wanted to keep it but 30 shillings was a lot of money. What I would give to have it today for a keepsake. One time I went for a dress fitting and in the distance I heard music from a carnival in a nearby field. I went over to the carnival and they were having a singing contest and I entered it and won 10 shillings. The winner was picked by the applause and it so happened a lot of my school friends were there and they went wild applauding for me. Another time I won a pound for singing in the cinema on Christmas day. Again by applause. It pays to have a big following.

Name That Tune

There was this guy who stopped by our house every Sunday after mass and we would have a "name that tune" contest with him on the piano. He'd put out 5 pence and if we guessed the first song he played we could double our money and go on to the next round. They were a no brainer at first but as the prize got bigger the songs got harder. For some reason we never cashed in because he would play something no one ever heard of, probably made it up and we'd lose all our money. I don't remember anyone ever cashing in. The other ritual was to sit by the window in our kitchen and watch the style coming from mass on Sunday. It was like a fashion parade. We had to make sure the kitchen light was out or they'd see us through the lace curtains.

We had another character in our town who went around town ringing a bell when the water was being shut off. His shoes had holes cut out for his bunions. Whenever he stopped by for a cup of tea mammy would use an old cracked cup because nobody would drink after him. His backyard stunk because he killed animals by banging their heads against the wall. We were the second family on our street to get a TV, I was sixteen. It was a big coffin of a thing, came from my aunt's bar. We had two stations, BBC and UTV, both British stations. They broadcast from 2pm - 11pm and ended the night playing "God save the Queen". Daddy would make us turn it off as soon as that came on, God forbid we hum along with it. The kids in the neighborhood came over Saturday evening to watch Star Trek and on Monday nights all the grownups watched ballroom dancing with Victor Sylvester. I had dreams of becoming a ballroom dancer, or an ice skater or a singer, but needless to say none ever panned out. There was never any alcohol in our house except for a bottle of whiskey hidden upstairs and that was for medicinal purposes only. Whenever there was a flu going 'round my father heated up lemons, cloves and whiskey and make us drink it. It was supposed to sweat the cold out of us. The other ritual was a spoon of cod liver oil once a year for worms whether you needed it or not. It was good for what ailed you if you didn't lose your tastebuds after taking it. I never tasted anything so horrible, try it!

Daddy's Weakness

I don't want to discredit my father but he had a serious drinking problem and he spent most of his time in the pub. Granted he made money wheeling and dealing from a bar stool without ever setting eyes on the animal. Mammy claimed he educated the publican's kids. He got up every morning, shaved, dressed in shirt and tie, suit and hat and his big horse dealer boots and went downtown looking spiffy. He came home drunk at noon, slept it off and went back down town when the pubs re-opened from 5-10pm although they had a back room for after hour's drinking. Whenever we'd hear the dreaded footsteps in the hallway we'd cringe because we didn't know what kind of mood he'd be in. He'd swing the kitchen door open with that look in his eyes, we knew we were in for it and my mother usually got the brunt of it. Mammy would warn us to stay put on his armchair otherwise he'd fall asleep in it and she'd never be able to get him to bed. Other times she'd chase us upstairs so we wouldn't be in the middle of it but we could hear it all. Our heart broke for her. Alcohol just didn't agree with daddy, looking back he may have been hypoglycemic because he went crazy when he drank and took it out on us all especially mammy. We were called useless good for nothings, those were the compliments, there was worse. Poor thing, he was the perfect description of a street angel and a house devil.

After a bad episode mammy would send for the priest the following morning to come and talk to him while he was still in bed. He'd yes the priest to death and just get up and do the same thing all over again. She'd call the police whenever he didn't come home at closing time, the police station was on the Main Street next to the pubs, they knew what was going on. We had very steep stairs and she'd ask one of us to stand behind him going up the stairs drunk so he wouldn't fall backwards. He never fell, as my mother would say the devil takes care of his own. One time I borrowed his razor to shave my legs and underarms for a dance. He was sitting by the cabinet and I couldn't sneak it back and so I planned on returning it the next morning before he got up but I forgot all about it. When he went to look for it he accused Tom of taking it, the most likely candidate right! Tom denied it naturally and daddy gave him hell and here was I sitting there innocently listening to it all, feeling guilty but I sure as hell wasn't going to own up. I kept my mouth shut until it was safe to return it. Sorry Tom, I owe you one!

Daddy's Good Side

By this time I swore I'd never marry an Irishman because I thought of Irish women as slaves and the men as alcoholics, it was a man's world and I wasn't going to settle for it but what I didn't know was that we were the exception not the norm. We never brought friends home because we didn't want anyone to know what was going on. Other than the drink he was a good person. He'd stand in the doorway and wave to everyone and give us a penny for toffee going back to school. On Sunday we got four pennies for the matinee and a penny to spend. The matinees were always cowboys and Indians and war pictures. We had three grocery shops on our street so we ran back and forth buying sweets. So much for our teeth and dental hygiene wasn't a common practice. When we came home from the movies the front door was always locked. We didn't understand at the time but in looking back I think that's when babies were made. Actually I thought they were made when mammy and daddy went for walks out the road because it seemed a baby soon followed. In all fairness to daddy it was the custom for men to go out drinking in a pub at night while the women sat home. Women who set foot in a pub got a bad reputation and there were a few. Every few years daddy would get bleeding ulcers, he claimed it was mammy's cooking but I'm sure stout was more likely the culprit. We'd light the fire upstairs and sit around playing games and singing while daddy fixed jewelry or darned socks. I was amazed he could darn so well because we were just learning to do it at school. Those were happy times even though he was sick.

At one time a family friend named Frank stayed with us. I loved him, he took me everywhere. One time we were having cabbage for dinner. I hated cabbage, I couldn't even swallow it and daddy told me I wasn't getting up from the table until I finished it that there were starving children in Africa that would give anything to have it. I was crying and he picked me up and took me for a walk out the Dundalk Road. He let me walk on the broken wall and he held my hand so I wouldn't fall. He used to talk me downtown and he'd go down steps on the Main St. and be gone for quite awhile. It was a mystery to me what was going on down there. I later learned it was men's toilets. One morning I went running into his room to tell him Tom stole his decorations and he was hanging out of the bed. I didn't realize he was dead. I just know I never saw him again. We also had an aunt stay with us for awhile. She worked in the jam factory. She used to sneak a smoke every chance she got and daddy was dead against smoking. Whenever she'd hear his footsteps in the hallway she'd throw her cigarette into the fire. The first four of us never smoked, we were afraid daddy would kill us. He threatened he'd take the mouth off us if he ever caught us smoking. Obviously the next four weren't afraid because they were chain smokers by the time they were teenagers. None of our friends smoked so I guess that made it easy for us. You could choke on the smoke from the balcony at the Sunday matinee from the underage kids puffing away. You couldn't even see the tops of their heads over the seats.

Boys Will Be Boys

Gerard and a Scottish friend took an empty shoebox, tied a string to it and left it in the middle of the Dundalk Road and then hid in daddy's field. Whenever anyone got out of their car to see what it was the boys would pull the string. Somebody reported it to the cops because it was during the troubles and there had been an incident where a bomb had been placed in a shoebox on the road and a cop got injured. The cops chased the boys up the fields until they caught them and scared the daylights out of them at the police station threatening to put them in jail. That was nothing compared to what they faced when the cops brought them home. They meant no harm, they were just fooling around, they didn't know anything about the bomb incident in the north. Gerard refused to take community showers when he went to the Technical school. He told them he went crazy when water hit his head. It worked, he was excused.

Michael was another rascal, he hated school, he'd bribe Gerard with cigarettes to cover for him when he skipped school which was most of the time. He hid in the neighbor's loft and then met up with Gerard coming down the backyard at the end of the school day and both of them walked into the house like butter wouldn't melt in their mouths. That was until the truant officer came to our door one day and told daddy Michael hadn't been to school in weeks. Daddy was waiting for him when he came home from "school" that day. All hell broke loose but it ran off Michael like water off a duck. It became my job to walk him to school after that. He was a foot taller than me, it was so embarrassing, I don't think it phased him one bit. I'd never even been up to the boy's school before, it was like forbidden territory for girls. Well, Michael went in the front door and out the back. He'd have already taken off before I got down the boy's lane. The principal gave up on him and let him take care of their animals at the monastery during the school day. Another time daddy came down the back yard and saw the windows of an old junk car all fogged up. He opened the door and there was Michael puffing his brains out.

When he was a teenager he had a zephyr car and he and his cohorts were known as the zephyr 5. Mary car pooled with them to the dances, I can't imagine what she had in common with them, they were crazy and she was such a goody goody. He was a good looking kid and the girls all chased after him but he treated them like dirt, easy come, easy go. When he was younger he was scared to death of thunder and lightning. One time we had a terrible storm and he was nowhere to be found. Mammy sent us out in the storm knocking on doors looking for him. Hours later we found him under the bed fast asleep, hiding from the storm

Irene went to the commercial school which I would have loved to have done because as life would have it I went into the corporate world. Irene never had to work a day in her life, she had a wonderful husband, a cop from grannies, and they had four kids. When we were young we shared a bed and we'd draw a pretend line down the middle and God forbid either one cross it. Mammy used to shout up the stairs to get us to shut up singing and get to sleep but we just quieted down a little, then one night we heard a whistle. That was daddy's signal but we knew it couldn't be him because the pubs weren't closed yet so we kept on singing. Suddenly the bedroom door swung open, we saw his image in the mirror with a rolled up newspaper in his hand. He gave us a few whacks that was one of the few times he ever hit us, he just had to give us the look. Michael got his fair share of beatings, I often thought when that kid grows up he's going to leave home and he did, very young. Mammy didn't hit us either, I guess they figured we got enough at school.

An out of town girl started working in the grocery store across the street and we became the best of friends. There was one incident where daddy was coming down the street drunk. My friend and I were standing at granny's door laughing about something. Daddy must have thought we were laughing at him which I would never do but he came over and kicked me with his hard boots across the street. I thought maybe he heard something about me and a guy I was dating on the fly so I was afraid to ask. This guy had a reputation for starting fights at football games and he was written up every week in the local paper. Mammy asked what happened, he never answered so to this day I don't know why he did it. I just figured there were times when I deserved it and didn't get it so we were even.

My Dear Little Cousin

I had a two-year-old cousin who was drowned in a little drop of water in a barrel in granny's backyard. She used it to catch rain water for the flowers. I'd had a dream the night before that I was in the butchers and he was cutting up rats and there was blood all over the place. I was told that was the sign of a death and sure enough that same day my little cousin was drowned. His sister was watching him in Granny's backyard and he dropped a crust of bread into the barrel and tried to retrieve it but fell in and drowned. His mother was pregnant with another baby at the time. There were other signs; an aunt heard an owl hooting outside her house the week prior, a robin flew in my aunt's window, a blackbird flew low and hit the windshield of daddy's car and then my dream. All signs of a death.

A Merry Christmas

Christmas was fun in our house. We put up the Christmas tree in our living room Christmas Eve. and went to bed early because if Santa saw us he might not leave anything. In the early morning we would slide our feet down to the bottom of the bed to see if Santa had come yet but we were scared a mouse might bite our toes so we'd call Tom to check. Toys were left at the bottom of the bed then instead of under the Christmas tree. We woke up early Christmas morning and ran into mammy and daddy's room to show them what Santa brought. Daddy always seemed to know how to put the toys together, wish I had his skill when I had my kids. When we stopped believing in Santa at around 10 we didn't get any more toys just gloves or grown up things so we held out as long as we could and pretended we still believed in him. I wanted a doll on my last Christmas but instead got a China tea set that auntie Winnie bought which incidentally is still around somewhere. That was my last chance to get a doll, I was very disappointed. The boys got play guns and we'd chase each other around the block playing cowboys and Indians or cops and robbers.

The pubs were closed on Christmas day so daddy was home all day. We'd cook the turkey in granny's oven with a sheet of suet on top and run back and forth basting it and checking on it. We played snakes and ladders and bingo on Christmas night. When I got older I made the turkey stuffing after midnight mass on Christmas Eve. The house would be full, everyone stopping in after mass for a cup of tea. There was never drink served in our house, or a lot of Irish homes, a cup of tea made with loose tea leaves was the drink of the day. And sometimes it was so strong you could walk on it. I always liked the first cup. Some people had the gift of reading tea leaves. As a teenager I hated the week between Christmas and New Years and the season of Lent because there were no dances. Our show bands, the Royal, the Capital, and the Clipper Carlton etc went to America during lent, lucky them!

One year daddy played Santa Clause and rode around town in a pony and trap. It was considered bad luck to take the tree down before little

Christmas or the epiphany, but one year they took the town tree down early maybe because of the weather and it fell on top of someone. There you go, they'll believe in superstition the next time. Daddy went on the binge during lent and we hated it, we weren't used to him being around at night, that was gossip time for the women. He'd also catch up on polishing all the brass on the horse's harness. He was real good at braiding a horse's mane and tail, running strings through them, just like show horses. He could be a big softie sometimes, Mary said she saw him crying at the movie "Imitation of Life". It was the drink that made him crazy. The day after Christmas, St. Steven's day we had a mummer's parade. People would dress up, some had painted black faces and they marched through town playing tambourines and other instruments and dancing. I don't know where that tradition came from or where they came from, they weren't from our town but they went from town to town performing. It wasn't unusual to be sitting in your house and hear music coming down the street. It would be a band marching through the town, men in kilts playing bagpipes, thin whistles and drums. I never liked the bagpipes, they had an eerie sound. I can see why they used them to go into battle, they'd scare the living daylights out of anyone, almost like a Banshee. Prior to Christmas we'd go carol singing around town and the proceeds went to Unicef.

Halloween was another adventure, we didn't have trick or treat, trick only. We'd knock on people's doors and run away and hide. Auntie Winnie threw a big party for all the neighborhood kids. We had bobbing for apples, trying to bite into a hanging apple with our hands tied behind our back and fortune telling where everyone was going to cross the ocean during their lifetime, lucky guess! Auntie Winnie was so good to us.

Beauty Shop Time

Daddy cut our hair, he'd put a newspaper around our neck and cut it straight across in a line with our ears. We'd go away and cry when we looked in the mirror. Mary was the only one with long hair. I guess that was because she was such an unhappy child, she did have beautiful long hair though. When I got older I slept in rollers as did my generation, I don't know how but it was very important to have our hair nice. Later curling irons replaced the rollers. I never had long hair until I realized one time in my 40s, I'm all grown up now and daddy's not around any more, I can have long hair if I want to. And so I decided to let it grow down my back but it was wavy and a pain to blow dry and I wasn't used to managing long hair. I couldn't tie it back in a ponytail because I had big donkey ears even though I had the retarded one surgically pinned back in my thirties but they did a lousy job. So that was the end of my long hair. Speaking of my big ear one time a plastic surgeon told me he could fix it but first he'd have to submit a request to the insurance company. They came back saying it was cosmetic surgery and they wouldn't approve. The Dr. wrote back this was not plastic surgery it was a retarded ear. They approved and my head was wrapped up like a mummy for a week and it's still not perfect. I had just bought a used car at the time and when I took it through the car wash it leaked around the windows, I was half drowned. I went back to the dealership mummy wrap and all, I thought they'd think I was in a head on collision or at least feel sorry for me but instead they took out the contract, circled "not responsible for leaks" and sent me on my way. That's the last time I bought a car from them, so there!

I had visions of being a hair dresser along with a dozen other things. I practiced cutting and setting my aunt's hair, the same people who had their first communion money hidden under their mattress but wouldn't spend a penny on their hair. The plan was, Mary and I would be the hairdressers and Thecla would wash hair and sweep up. Of course that never materialized because we all left home. We had a community comb and it was kept on the mantlepiece so if one got lice we all got lice. Then out came the fine tooth comb to get rid of the lice. The dentist from the clinic came to our school once a year. If you had a toothache or a bad tooth out it came, no such thing as preventive care. We had a relative working in the clinic and she used to get us jars of malt which we loved, it was supposed to build us up.

Irish Cures

There were lots of cures in those days. One was the cure for mumps. The story goes that if you put a donkey's blinkers on the person and walk them up and down our backyard repeating mucna, mucna, lecna, lecna, cure these mumps of mine, the mumps would go away. My brother Tom had it done, I don't know if it worked but every kid with mumps had the ritual performed in our back yard. Maybe it was the yard. Another cure was the warts, only certain people had the cure, they used ten straws tied with a red thread and said ten Our Fathers, one with each straw, buried nine of them and threw the last one over their shoulder. The warts were supposed to die when the buried straws died. I had it done but it didn't work. I was told it's because I didn't believe hard enough, whatever! I suffered from headaches when I was young, some real, some fake to stay home from school and granny Clarke would say it's "it". I never knew what "it" was but in hindsight I think she was referring to puberty. Daddy took me to Monaghan hospital for X-rays, apparently my brain was intact, then I went to a priest with the cure for headaches and he prayed over me and I very rarely ever get a headache today. I had an uncle with the cure for shingles, they say he mixed the ashes from blessed palms with the blood of a rooster's cone and rubbed it on the shingles, the jury's out on that one. There was a woman in our town who was the seventh daughter of the seventh daughter and she had the cure for burns. It just so happens she had a baby that was scalded to death in a bathtub of boiling water.

My uncle worked in a garage and he accidentally threw a lit match into a barrel of petrol and it exploded and burned him all over. Granny brought him to this woman and she healed him, he didn't have a scar left on his body. They said she soaked the bark of a certain tree in water and rubbed it on the burns. I know her cure worked, he didn't have a mark on him, I saw it for myself. It didn't stop him from smoking though. We always sang along with the radio and he would tell us to hush up, he could hear us anytime. Then there was the Banshee. A ghost like figure who followed certain families. She had long hair, dressed in white and wailed when a death was near. People swear they saw her when our neighbor died. I lived across the street but I didn't see or hear anything. Later I heard a noise that could be mistaken for a Banshee but it was cats in heat. Every time I went to Crossmaglen it seemed some baby had thrush in their mouth. The cure was to rub the inside of their mouth with a wet diaper. Don't confuse these cures with Irish superstitions because we don't believe in leprechauns or the pot of gold although I'd like to find one, or the black cat crossing our path as good luck or stunting our growth if we walk under a ladder.

Auntie Minnie And Music

Daddy had a blind sister, auntie Minnie. She played the piano and sang and whenever she came to our house on vacation we'd all get together around the piano in our living room and have a good old ceili. The neighbors passing by would hear us and drop in for the craic and a cup of tea. I swear she knew every song that was ever written. She also gave piano lessons, she taught me a few songs but that's the extent of my music ability. I could never play anything on my own. I took piano lessons in school but I wanted to be able to play by ear. I can do it with one hand but not both. I can't read music for the right and left hand and then locate the keys for both hands on the piano at the same time. Talk about multi-tasking. My mind doesn't work that way. It's like walking and chewing gum x 10. My aunt could identify a person by their footstep, their voice or touching their face. She could hear a pin drop. Tom sang at midnight mass one time and it was beautiful but he lost his voice right after (that puberty thing again). He used to lock himself in the living room for hours learning to play the piano, we thought he was getting odd. He emerged from the living room a year later a new man, he got his voice back and sang like Mario Lanza and could play the piano like a pro. A miracle! That was the time I was trying to break the ice going to dances.

We had a high school principal, who ran the choir and the local plays in our Catholic hall every year. Everyone who could sing or dance was in those plays. One time we sang "it's a long way to Tipperary" and somebody started booing and throwing things up on the stage. We didn't know that was a British recruiting song. Auntie Minnie played the piano at our concerts. Irene and I sang duets, we were the Clarke sisters, later on Mary and I performed together. I also did Irish dancing. After years of competing in Feises (Irish competitions) I ended up with only one medal for singing and one for dancing. The judges saw me year after year, they probably thought I was the teacher.

Tom took over the choir after the H.S. principal died and trained a local group to compete in talent shows all over the country, he even made the scenery himself. The whole family participated except Irene and I, we were already left home by then. Mammy and daddy travelled all over with them, they were so proud. Then Tom started a country and western band called the Presidents with Mary as the lead singer, Samantha was her stage name. I missed out on all of that, I would have loved it.

Summer Vacations In Crossmaglen

Irene and I spent our summer vacations at Granny Clarkes in Crossmaglen. Daddy drove us over in a horse and trap. Irene hung out at an aunts babysitting her kids while I hung out at Grannies helping out in the shop. The first thing Granny did was check our hair for lice and bring us to the clinic because she always thought we were undernourished just because we were skinny, I made up for it later. The cure was a jar of malt which we were already taking. One time when Michael was about 6 he came with us but when it came bedtime there was no way in hell he was going to bed. He cried so much they had to call daddy & he had to come back and get him. I just had a similar experience with my new dog, Bailey. I left him over my grand daughters' and he wouldn't stop crying, I had to go pick him up at 10pm.

Granny churned her own ice cream. She stood outside her store on Fridays with a big barrel of herrings shouting "herrings alive". People picked out their herrings and she wrapped them in newspaper. Fish and chips were also wrapped in newspaper and it didn't do us a bit of harm. I think the world has gone crazy with over sanitizing, we built up our immune system playing in dirt, bathing once a week, dampness running down the walls, sleeping on DDT sprayed mattresses and wiping our butts with newspaper. Then there were the flies and the wasps buzzing around everywhere, hospitals, restaurants, kitchen tables, landing on our food because people opened their windows for fresh air and there were no screens. Fifty years later they still don't have screens.

Want Some Smuggled Goods?

This brings me to the smuggling. Granny Clarke had a store in the north where butter was cheaper and granny Allen had a restaurant in the south where cigarettes were cheaper. There was a border between the north and the south and granny Clarke and her daughters would smuggle butter under their clothes coming over on the bus and they'd smuggle cigarettes going back. My aunts were very heavy so I don't know how they hid anything under their clothing. I don't know how they got away with it because the customs men used to inspect the bus for smuggled goods. They even involved my poor blind aunt in their smuggling scheme. Granny Allen kept lodgers, some of them policeman. She mixed the butter with margarine to make it stretch further and they'd joke about how good the butter was knowing it was smuggled. Granny Clarke kept the smuggled cigarettes with the free state stamp on them under the store counter for "preferred" customers. Goats and other livestock were smuggled between the north and the south by going across the fields avoiding the border. After the peace treaty the borders were taken down but now that Britain has gotten out of the European Union (Brexit) the borders have become an issue again, how to deal with goods coming from north to south and vise versa. I always imagined how my granny's advice to their daughters at marriage would have differed, one would say " make sure you break your man in right from the beginning and let him know who's boss" while the other's advice would be "be good to your man, treat him right". I think the best advice lay somewhere in between.

Some Not So Good Memories

I have two really bad memories of my childhood, one where a man chased me around the kitchen and tried to put his hands up my clothes and touch me in forbidden places. He didn't only do it once, he tried it every time we were alone. A lot of men got a kick out of touching young girls on the boobs when they were developing, they thought it was funny and they got away with it because we were too scared to tell. Another was a family friend who invited me out the road to plant flowers while the owners were on vacation. I lived in the town and I'd never planted flowers so I went with him on the handlebars of his bicycle. He locked the shed, sat down and unzipped his pants and asked me to touch him. I tried to escape and fortunately my friend caught up with us and rescued me. Next day at school I learned he'd done it before to another girl but her father went to the police and he got in trouble. Once again I blamed myself for going with him. I never told on either one because I thought daddy would kill me or them. The guy still came around our house but I watched him like a hawk, I had four younger sisters. In hindsight I wish I'd told my parents because I worried about my siblings after I left home. I wrote a letter to Mary and told her what happened and asked her to watch out for Regina. Funny, I didn't worry about him doing anything to Thecla because I knew she'd clobber him. Later he befriended Michael and I worried that he might be gay, he never married. Michael later assured me nothing happened that he just liked hanging out at his house because his sister taught him to read and write. I had my doubts he was telling the truth. I sent a draft of this book to my sisters and discovered they had similar experiences but with different men, and it took this book to bring all our secrets out in the open. What a shame, sickos!

Lesson for my girls: Try not to put yourself in a situation where you are alone with an older man especially if you can't defend yourself, bring a friend. Always let someone know where you're going. Don't blame yourself if something happens, you didn't do anything wrong, he did. Don't be afraid to expose him otherwise he's likely to do it to somebody else. Understand there's some bad people out there and they can be the ones you least expect. Watch out for your children also.

Kathy Kelly

Traditions

Daddy cooked the Sunday breakfast while the girls were at the 9am mass. He'd sing all the old Irish songs while he fried bacon, eggs, black and white pudding and fried bread soaking up all that good bacon grease (no wonder we have ulcers). As I got older I helped out and we sang together. I wasn't familiar with the songs because we mostly listened to top 20 hits but I learned them from him. His favorites were "The Bridle Hanging on the Wall and The Old Bog Road".

A big tradition was to go to the beach on August 15th. the feast of the Assumption for the blessing of the waters. Incidentally that was Michael and Thecla's birthday. All ten of us piled into a little Volkswagen bug to spend the day at Blackrock. The tide was always way out so all we got was seaweed wrapped around our ankles, besides none of us could swim anyway. We'd sit on the wall at the beach all afternoon while daddy went to the pub. Then we rode home with him swerving all over the road, mammy was scared to death but we were singing away in the back seat except for an odd woops and we'd fall on top of each other, we thought it was fun, we didn't realize we could have all been killed. Our guardian angel was watching over us. Another tradition was to go to confessions Good Friday, make the stations of the cross before 3pm and whatever you asked for God granted your wish. One time I did all of that and asked for a pair of white sandals with toes and heels out for Easter and I got them the next day. Not sure if that's what God had in mind.

On weekends all the teenagers hung out at the chip shop with the juke box. We'd split a plate of chips between us and move from table to table until they hired a new manager. If we changed tables she expected us to make another purchase. We were school kids for Pete's sake, we had no money, we weren't there to spend money we were there to match make. That was our match.com. That's where all the teen romances began and ended up in the hay barn. I want you to know going to the hay barn was harmless, we went there because we couldn't afford to go anywhere else.

The North And Catholicism

Daddy came from the north where it was hard being catholic because they were in the minority and the underdogs, they had no rights. Protestants were in the majority and ne'er the two should mix. The same was true in the republic where the catholics were in the majority. I'm married to a northerner and I find them to be much more patriotic than the free state because they had to fight to keep their Irish culture and their catholic religion alive. They were not taught Gaelic in school or allowed to use Gaelic names for their children. My husband's family wanted to call him Sean but because it was Gaelic for John they had to put John on the birth certificate. They called him Sean anyway. Most Catholics in the north had big families. They were subservient to the Protestants who owned most of the property and only property owners were allowed to vote. The British governed the north and they evicted the Catholics living on rich soil and moved in Protestants from England and Scotland. The Catholics had to migrate to the west of Ireland where farming was next to impossible because of the rocky land. Throughout the years there have been troubles between the north and the south and it is hoped that one day we will have a united Ireland. The tables have turned and now Catholics are in the majority because of the big catholic families. They're calling for a referendum to decide whether the occupants want to remain under British rule or join the Republic. It's unbelievable but some Catholics would prefer to stay with the British for the benefits.

Religion and The Changes In The South

The Republic of Ireland has become very liberal in recent years. They were the first European country to legalize abortion. Imagine, the Island of saints and scholars legalizing abortion. It goes against everything the Catholic Church teaches. The young people don't go to church and suicide is very prevalent. I'm sure St. Patrick, would roll over in his grave as would our ancestors. Child molestation by priests has done the church a lot of damage. We had a priest in our town that everybody loved but all of a sudden he was transferred to a country parish. He coached the boy's football team and had them stay overnight. Later we found out he was a pervert. Baby's remains were found in drains on the property of a Catholic orphanage in the west of Ireland. People felt betrayed, the priests were like God, the church was God's house, they could do no wrong or so we thought. Even the older generation has stopped going to mass which is inexcusable.

You go to mass to honor God not the priests, God didn't do anything wrong, his earthly representatives did. I'm sure God is very angry and disappointed in these people for tarnishing His image. Who do people turn to in time of need? I lost a daughter and a husband and I don't know how I would have survived if I didn't have God to lean on. I feel the immigrants held on to their religion better than those who stayed behind. At home we went to church because somebody noticed if we were missing. When we left home we went because we wanted to, because we loved God and had a good catholic foundation. We grew up saying the rosary every night. We tried to get it said before auntie Winnie arrived because she recited the litany of the saints which took forever. My mother claimed the family that prays together stays together. I thought that meant we'd all stay close to home when we grew up but we're scattered between America, Wales and the east coast of Ireland.

We had a beautiful big church on our street with one of the highest spires in the country. The church chimes rang out "the bells of the angeles" at noon and 6 pm every day. People stopped in their tracks, blessed themselves and silently prayed the angelus. Funerals passed by our house almost every evening at about 7 o'clock. You would hear the church bells ringing (the death toll) followed by the procession passing our house on the way to the church. We'd run out and close the front door which was usually left open and turn out all the lights out of respect for the dead. We also had this tradition in our church to pay offerings at a funeral so no matter who died daddy seemed to know them and if he couldn't be there someone had to represent him and pay his offering. The priest would read out loud the name of the person making the offering and how much they paid. In later years it was abolished, I thought it was awful it was like putting a price on a dead man's head, how many friends they had and how much they were worth. Wakes were another story, there was no embalming then. The corpse was dressed in a brown shroud and laid out at home on the first night and the church the next night. Family and friends stopped by for the wake which consisted of prayer, food and alcohol. It was a big strain on a family, you were so busy catering to the visitors you didn't have a chance to spend time with the deceased. That's an ancient tradition thank God.

We had a procession to the Blessed Virgin every May. People dressed up their front windows with a statue of Mary, candles and flowers. The priest led the procession around town carrying a statue of the blessed Virgin while praying and singing hymns followed by benediction in the church. They still do it today, however because of Covid-19 only the priest and my brother Tom walked in the procession this year. We also had a mission once a year where a missionary priest visited. They were usually great preachers. Stalls were set up on the church grounds where they sold religious souvenirs like scapulars, novenas, and rosary beads. Mostly old people wore scapulars because they'd show under our clothes and the boys might think we were holy rollers. That would scare them away.

Our Daily Mutton

Daddy bought sheep and split them with granny for the restaurant. We had a butcher friend who cut them up. I had zits as a teenager and daddy claimed if I drank lamb's blood it would purify my blood. I wasn't going to find out, that was gross. Whenever we complained of having lamb chops daddy would say "one day you'll eat the hand of the person giving them to you". He must have been a prophet because I wouldn't spend the money on them today they're so expensive. Sometimes we ate goats, venison, God knows what else. Whenever we asked what we were eating daddy would say "just eat it and be glad you have it". It didn't seem to do us any harm, we were all pretty healthy. Every year mammy bought two pigs who had little piglets and when she sold them at the auction that was her pocket money. I remember coming home from school one day and there was a little pig wrapped in a blanket sitting on the oven door. It seemed he was the weakling of the family and mammy was trying to keep him alive. It was like a little baby, little did he know we were just raising him to end up on someone's dinner table. Dogs and cats ran the streets. Every time a car came down our street our dog Spot chased after it, it was his downfall, he ended up getting killed by one when he was fifteen years old.

A cousin and I rented bikes and rode to Crossmaglen which was about 9 miles away. One time we were coming home when we got a flat tire and it was getting late so we stopped at a farm house for help. They knew daddy of course, it seemed everyone knew Mick Clarke especially around the border so they fixed the tire and gave us a cup of tea and we were on our way. By the time we got home mammy was worried sick. Another time we rode 13 miles to Dundalk. That was a long ride, we never did it again. Very few people had house phones in those days except the old maids next door. They had a pay phone on their living room wall. Grannie Clarke called us there once in a while and they'd come and get us. Daddy would warn us "for God's sake don't ask her how she's doing or she'll take up the whole call telling you about her aches and pains".

The first Thursday of every month was the fair day in our town and all the farmers brought their livestock to town to sell. They sealed the deal with a spit and a hand shake. So much for hygiene! The horses were tied up on the street outside everyone's front door. I was afraid running between them for fear of them kicking me. Granny's restaurant was very busy on fair days, we spent hours buttering loaves of sliced bread the evening before. We never went to school on a fair day and rather than tell the nuns the truth we said we were sick, like they didn't know. By the way, there were no tips then so it wasn't like we were working for money. Mammy got paid in butter. Granny snuck the rest over to us. Even though the restaurant was grannys, my aunt ran it so she was the boss.

School Days

One time we were doing a school operetta, the Gondoliers. I was in fifth grade and I was to play a princess and sing a solo. I went for the dress fitting and the next day I was told another girl was going to be princess but I still had the solo. My replacement was much prettier than I and my feelings were crushed, I always knew I was no beauty queen but that confirmed it. We performed in the Catholic hall and one of the nuns played the piano. She reported back every morning to the nun who directed us and we went into school each morning never knowing what to expect. There were several times when we thought we had done a good job but apparently we didn't smile enough or sing loud enough or some other petty thing so we got slapped. That took all the good out of what could've been a great experience.

The one and only time I ever cheated at school I got caught. I hadn't studied for an exam and the girl sitting next to me was a pure genius. I took a peek at one of her answers and apparently so did the girl the other side of her and the answer was wrong. So now all three of us had the same wrong answer. I think she did it on purpose so we got called up and whacked. I agree I deserved it that time.

I won a scholarship to the boarding school otherwise we would never have been able to afford it. I got a hand me down uniform from our neighbor and was embarrassed when we went to show ourselves off to our seventh grade nun, everyone had a new uniform and mine was all faded. Everything was taught in Gaelic and we had to translate it into English in our mind to understand it. I learned French, Latin, science and algebra through Gaelic. What baloney, it wasn't like Gaelic was our first language but that's how things were done then, you got extra points in exams for using Gaelic, big deal! You had to be fluent in Gaelic to join the cops. Now what drunk do you know who fights in Gaelic, it's usually the f...n language. Granted we have parts of Ireland where Gaelic is their first language, it's called the Gaeltach. You had to be able to sing to be a teacher, isn't that ridiculous. There were kids from all over Ireland at the boarding school, the local townies were day girls so we went to school from 9-3pm and then back to study from 5-7pm. We even had school Saturday morning. I think the nun's goal was to convert the boarders to nuns because they got up praying and went to bed praying. I'm not sure how successful they were because they certainly didn't make it very enticing. I told my math teacher I wanted to be a bookkeeper so she took me aside and showed me little tricks about adding up that sure came in handy when I finally started working. I thought I had a vocation to be a nun. I went to mass every morning and whenever I closed my eyes I saw an image of a nun in a white African habit. I prayed to God to take this calling away because I wanted to marry and have kids, and He did. Later in life I got a chance to serve Him.

Our "Favorite" People, The Nuns

Whenever we greeted a nun on the street we had to say "go mbeannaithe Dia dhuit" (God's blessings on you), they responded "Dia is Muire dhuit" (God and Mary's blessing on you), that was the only time we spoke Irish out of school. Most of the time we tried to duck the nuns. There was one however, sister Mary Thecla who auntie Winnie befriended. The story goes she joined the convent because she wanted to be a nurse but they were a teaching order and she ended up working in the kitchen. She was the only nun that wasn't intimidating. Incidentally my sister Thecla was named after her and I've never met anyone else with that name. An old lodger in grannys couldn't say her name so he called her Hitler. That name stuck for the longest time. Of course we didn't know who Hitler was back then.

Poor Regina had some bad experiences with the nuns. I later found out that while taking piano lessons her teacher, a nun of course, was angry and slammed the lid of the piano down on her fingers. The poor kid was in shock. Sister Mary Thecla had snuck in that day unnoticed to hear her play and witnessed the whole thing. She picked Regina up off the piano stool and took her home crying, her knuckles bleeding. They're disfigured to this day and she has arthritis in them. Another time she took a day off school to see me off at the airport. The principal had refused her the day off but daddy insisted she come. Next day when she went to school the principal was behind the door and slammed it in her face knocking her unconscious. She had to be sent home. My father who had never been to the school in his life went up there fit to kill and whatever he said to the nun she never touched Regina again. Poor kid, she had worse luck with the nuns than any of us. One time I was taking singing lessons and the nun shook me to put some life into me, she said I was too dead. She must have been watching Elvis shake rattle and roll.

A four year old boy in kindergarten spilled a box of matches on his first day of school. The principal beat him to a pulp. His mother took him and showed him to the Monsignor and the police. The church ruled the roost, they got away with murder, they ran the police and the town. Thank God that has all changed and today's kids don't have to go through the nightmare that we went through. Legally you had to be fourteen to leave school in those days and most kids were out the door the minute they turned fourteen. If school had been more pleasant kids might have stayed longer. After primary school the next step was to go to commercial class, the boarding or technical school, get a job in one of the local factories and get married and raise a bunch of kids or immigrate if you were fortunate enough to have relatives to claim you. In America they had to provide proof that they could support you financially until you got a job so you wouldn't be a burden on the country. The average family couldn't afford any higher education, those spots were reserved for the lawyers and doctor's kids regardless of their academic status.

Let's Twist Again

We were a big family but we didn't hang out together as teens, we each had our own friends. We had the usual sibling squabbles as kids especially Mary and I over clothes. One time I was going to a dance and couldn't find my dress. I found it on Mary sitting watching TV in a shop across the street. One time I borrowed her fur hat for the movies and sneaked it back before she got home. Today she would give you the clothes off her back. I had a sleeveless red brocade dress for the dances. One week I wore it sleeveless, the next I sewed see through sleeves in it and vise versa. It was like having 2 separate outfits. We also knitted our own sweaters, one Friday I remember finishing off a white sweater for the dance. It was a button down the back, that was the style then. We had some great ceilis in grannys. We'd pull back all the tables and chairs in the dining room, one of the cops played the accordion, another the fiddle and the rest of us danced and sang.

Come On Let's Dance

I went to my first dance with one of the policemen staying in Grannys who incidentally married my sister Irene later on. My mother had said I couldn't go, her rationale was once I started there would be no stopping me. I took my chances anyway and ended up next to her on the floor after the first dance. She was shocked, I told her daddy said I could go. She was correct in her predictions because that was the beginning of the end. I was dance crazy. In the beginning I had to be home by midnight, like Cinderella, it wasn't fair, the dance wasn't over 'til one but I had to beat daddy home from the pub. One night he beat me home but I saw him first. So I had to come down the back yard in the dark, scared of a mouse or rat jumping out in front of me. Olive wasn't a very common name then and when a guy would ask me my name on the dance floor with the show band blasting in the background they'd think I said Alice so I'd say Olive, as in Popeye. Oh, I got it Alice, whatever!

Later Irene and I slept in grannys because auntie Winnie went to America and granny needed company. I got dropped off up the street at 3am. after a Kingscourt dance and ran down to grannys in my pantyhose in case daddy heard me across the way. Then there was the very distinct click of her front door. I thought I got away with it but years later I heard him tell someone "Olive thought I didn't know what was going on". Whenever I was going out and him standing in the front doorway which he did a lot, I'd throw my clothes out the back window and sneak out the back way. I don't know if he would have objected but I never asked, I just assumed he wouldn't let me go. If only my older brother Tom danced he would have broken the ice for me and I wouldn't have had to sneak around. I took Tom to his first dance and taught him to dance. It was easy, he had the rhythm. It was a carnival and he stuck to me like glue the whole night, everyone thought I was on a date. Once a drunk guy asked me to dance and I said I wasn't dancing, so he said "where's your f....n knitting". I rarely ever refused a dance because I thought it took a lot of courage for a guy to walk across a floor and ask a girl, I even danced with a midget not to hurt his feelings.

From the time I was sixteen my favorite pastime was dancing just like a lot of teens from my generation. We had the local Catholic hall on Friday nights and the Granada in Kingscourt on Sunday. Kingscourt was the best but we had to chip in for a taxi to go there. We sat on each other's laps sometimes six to a taxi. The first thing we asked a guy on the dance floor was how did you get here. If it was a bike or a ride forget it! We needed a guy with a car. If you didn't have a date, the girls stood on one side of the floor and the boys on the other. As soon as the music started the guys charged across the floor, grabbed a girl and took off. If you were one of the unfortunates to be left standing after the stampede you wished you could crawl into a hole and die. Then there were the duty dances by friends and family. They were a waste of precious time because we weren't interested in them. Then came ladies choice, where the tables were turned and the girls got to pick the guys. Sometimes a guy would refuse you and you'd pick someone next to him rather than be embarrassed walking back across the floor. The smokers always looked like they could care less if they got chosen or not, they just puffed away so I tried a puff but I started coughing and my nose running. That was the end of smoking for me for life. There was no alcohol served at our dances, just minerals but a lot of the guys didn't arrive until the pubs closed so we knew they had a few drinks in them. We had the saying "did you click or did you lift or did you hook up" meaning did you get a guy.

Mammy and daddy were beautiful dancers. When we were young daddy danced with us to the radio. Then he'd say "you don't know how to dance" and he'd pick Mammy up and they'd waltz around the kitchen floor. It looked so hard I thought I'm never gonna be able to dance like that. Little did I know very few people danced like that, that was ballroom dancing. I actually won a dance contest one time in the Catholic hall. I wasn't that good but my partner was. I think he just asked me because all the good dancers were taken. It took me awhile to pick up the rhythm of the twist. Myself and a few friends practiced in a room over her father's bar until we got it down pat. It was a good dance if you didn't want to be seen with your partner or if he couldn't dance. Once Mammy was in the hospital with a miscarriage. After giving birth to nine kids at home she was now in hospital for the first time. It was strange her not being home, we were lost without her, the house wasn't the same. I'm sorry for the kids who don't have a mother there when they come home from school, including my own. It was so comforting to know she would always be there. She was always happy, singing and dancing. She was soft spoken, Mary has her personality. I surprised her and made curtains for the kitchen window while she was away. It was my first time and I forgot to allow for the hem and I know she paid a lot for the material. She never complained.

Granny had two sisters in America. One married a cancer research doctor and whenever his work took him to Europe they always stopped in to see her. We'd dance and sing and entertain them just like we did all visitors. One time they gave us each a Kennedy half dollar. We couldn't wait for the bank to open the next day to cash them in. I was a bit disappointed, they weren't worth as much as I had expected. Maybe they thought we'd keep them as souvenirs, no way!

A rumor started that the time had come for the pope to open a sealed letter from the three children of Fatima. The media had everyone in a frenzy. As luck would have it we had a big power outage in our town that day, the street lights were out, it was dark outside even in the middle of the day which was creepy. All the signs of doom and gloom were there. Everyone was terrified, we thought it was the end of the world. Guess what, when the pope opened the letter it was a bill for the last supper. What a prank to play on everyone.

My Teenage Dating Years

I dated a few guys during my teens. One joined the Irish army around the time "send me the pillow that you dream on" by Bobby Vinson came out so that was our song. We wrote back and forth for awhile but then things went cold. As my mother would say "faraway hearts are soon forgotten" but would you believe I went out with his younger brother once. I never dated younger guys, I was more attracted to the older ones and this one didn't change my mind. Most kids didn't have money to go on a date so we went to the hay barn. All my friends used it, you never knew who you were going to "bump" into. My biggest fear was rats or mice jumping out of the hay. Well the "baby" and I went there on our date. My friend picked the hay off me before I got home and I told her I was never going out again with a younger guy, he didn't even know how to kiss. Boy was I wrong, he was trying to French kiss, I was the dummy. I later dated the guy who's family owned the hay barn but he wasn't a dancer, needless to say that didn't last long. I met another guy who gave me a hickey. I went into work the next day when someone noticed it, I'd never had a hickey before so I didn't even know what one looked like. I had to wear turtlenecks until it wore off. The nerve of the little brat!

I was never out of my hometown much except to go to the dances in Kingscourt or Castleblayney. I was only in Dublin a few times, once for my first Holy Communion dress, then for my passport and lastly on a legion of Mary outing. We were supposed to go to the Dublin zoo but we ended up at the Metropole. The lighting was psychedelic, a first for us country bumpkins and there were all colors of people, another first. It was very scary, I was only 17 and these people were much older. I couldn't wait to get out of there. It was as hard to get to Dublin as it was America in those days. We might have only one bus running and it could take hours to get there with the narrow roads and farmers walking their cows or sheep to the fields. You couldn't pass them so you had to wait until they got to their destination. Also we had no relatives in Dublin to bunk in with.

Carrickmacross lace is made in our hometown and it's famous all over the world. It was originally made by a few nuns in the convent but they were getting old and they didn't want it to die out with them so they opened it up to the townspeople. I joined the class with a few friends, made a little centerpiece and started a wedding veil. I figured I'd have it done by the time I got married especially since I had no prospects at the time. Well needless to say I never finished it, I don't even know what happened to it. Bing Crosby's wife used to buy a lot of lace. Mary's friend designs and runs the operation today.

My Fist Romance

The love of my teens was Danny boy. He came from a big family and they all had nicknames. From the time I was 16 to 18 my life was consumed by him. He was a few years older and he had a car so now I didn't have to pay for a taxi anymore. Cars were a luxury in those days so if you hooked a guy with a car that was a big catch. We went to a matinee on our first date, Ben Hur was playing, not a very romantic movie to start off a first date. We went out a few times and I was crazy about him but obviously the feeling wasn't mutual because he let me down one time. I got Thecla to come with me and we sat in his car outside a pub waiting for him. I blush just thinking how brazen I was, he wasn't getting off that easy. He was shocked to see me but he took me to the dance anyway and that was the end of our romance. He just dropped me off after the dance and said goodnight, no follow up date. I was heartbroken. I'd sit home crying with my friend, as I listened to "are you lonesome tonight" by Jim Reeves. I'd walk out to the football field with my aunt just to see him practice football. I didn't know the first thing about football, still don't, we were into music not sports. He started dating another girl and I started dating a guy mostly so I could go to the places he went. I guess you'd call that stalking today. I spent the next two years dreaming of him asking me out again.

One week before I was due to leave home my dream came true, Danny boy asked me out. We went to the movies in Dundalk and on the way home we parked by the convent lake. He laid me down in the front seat of his car and got up on top of me. We usually sat up necking but I thought laying down, sitting up, what's the difference but then I felt something sticking into me and I asked him if he had a pen in his pocket. He said "are you sure it's a pen", it wasn't until I left home that I discovered what that pen was but I didn't know it could grow. You're reading about a girl who believed a co-worker who said you could get pregnant without having sex. That the man could get excited and it could crawl up your leg and get you pregnant. That the term "virgin" only applied to the blessed virgin. If Danny boy had shown up at the airport and asked me to stay I would never have left. He later married a local girl and became very successful in business during the boom. I guess I missed the boat there, wonder what would have happened if I'd let him write with that pen, God forgive me. I saw him years later and I wondered what I ever saw in him. It was just a teenage crush that consumed my life, stupid me! Amazing how time changes everything.

Leaving Home

I was the last person anyone ever expected to leave home. I was too close to my mother, I was a real homebody. I dreamed of marrying a local guy, living up the street and dropping in to see my mother every day with my kids but that was not to be. I wanted to be a nurse and the only way I could do that was to go to England to get my RN because you got free training, free housing and a small stipend, then I was coming back home and working in a local hospital. You had to pay for training and housing in Ireland and we couldn't afford it. That's their loss, I know I would have made a good nurse. A friend of mine had gone to nursing school in England so I got all the paperwork and had everything ready to go.

My father having come from the north swore none of his kids were ever going to set foot on British soil so I waited for the right time to ask him. It never came. Incidentally Thecla went off to Wales later and became a nurse but never came back to live. I was home on vacation the day she left without telling anyone. Someone told daddy they saw her getting on a bus to Dublin. He went ballistic, he even went to the police station to get them to intervene but they said they couldn't do anything because she was 18. God love her, I don't know where she got the courage to go off alone but she made it and nursed until she retired.

Auntie Winnie, my mother's sister, (the one who said the litany of the saints) had gone to America a few years earlier and got a job working as a housekeeper for a doctor, a widower. She sent home packages of clothes for us including shorts and the Sunday funnies. We never wore shorts in public at that time, just in the house or out back. We'd change to go outside or to answer the front door. We'd send pictures to her of us wearing the clothes, a good incentive for more, right! Granny went out to visit her, it was the first time I ever saw Granny with short hair, she wore it in a bun as long as I could remember. When she came home she was bragging about the great country America was. She said she was in a bank one day and they were closing up at 2 o'clock, she said you could be a millionaire, you could have two jobs. She offered me the opportunity to go and she would pay my way, so I took her up on the offer.

I applied for my passport and it was then that I learned the name Olivia was not on my baptismal or birth certificate. I'd been called Olive all my life, now what! I don't know if it was the priest or my god parents that left it off maybe they didn't like Olivia deHavilland, remember we were baptized at three days while our mother was still recovering from child birth. God forbid we die without being baptized and go to Limbo which is no more. And to top it off I was Catherine on my baptismal and Katherine on my birth certificate. Mary and Irene had their birth days reversed. I guess it's hard to keep up with so many kids. I don't even remember calendars being around then. When I went to the police station for my clearance, the policeman asked me how tall I was. I said I don't know, he stood next to me and said, I'm 5'10, you're about 5'2 and so I became 5'2 for the rest of my life without ever measuring myself.

AMERICA, HERE I COME!

On the morning of my departure I went around saying goodbye to all the neighbors. It was January and the roads were very icy and there was no such thing as a snow plough. All the old ladies gave me a keepsake of a broach and pinned it on my new suede jacket. Mammy didn't come to Dublin airport because she got car sick. I remember shaking daddy's hand goodbye, God forbid a man show any sign of affection and break down crying. Tom and Regina hugged me. A girl from my school was a stewardess on the Air Lingus flight and another family from my town was on the same flight but I never saw them again. We got a write up in the Democrat, the local newspaper. We were celebrities! Actually when I was a kid the editor told me he was going to marry me when I grew up. He was old enough to be my father. He used to visit the old maids next door. I was broken hearted leaving Mammy and Regina, she was only 8 years old and my shadow, wherever I went she went. She even slept with me. Since I worked for a shoe factory and wore the sample size 4 I had lots of free samples of pointy toe stiletto heels so I packed them all in a carry on covering up some Irish bacon and sausages I was smuggling. When I went through customs they asked what was in the bag, I said shoes, they said you must intend to do a lot of walking in America.

First Impressions

I remember flying over the Statue of Liberty. I can imagine how that must have felt to our ancestors who came to America to escape famine, war and poverty. Coming to the land of opportunity. The lights below were breathtaking. I thought I was seeing the whole of America at one time. The band mustn't have gotten the memo, they were not there to greet me. In the airport I noticed a woman struggling with suitcases and men were just rushing past her. I thought the age of chivalry must be dead in America. Little did I know you couldn't trust anyone to help you, welcome to America! Auntie Winnie and an American cousin I'd never met before were there to greet me. He said "you'll do fine in America, you just have to shed some of the jewelry". I looked down and realized I had five broaches on my jacket from the old ladies back home. We had tea and I was shocked you had to leave a tip. We never tipped in Ireland, I thought it's the employer's job to make up the waitress' salary not the customer. We took the Garden State Parkway to NJ, I couldn't believe roads could be so wide, I was used to country roads and no lights in Ireland. I saw my cousin drop a coin in a basket going through what I learned was a toll booth. Again I thought, OMG, you have to pay to use the roads in America. I was in for a whole new awakening. Then we stopped for gas, the sign read 31.9 cents per gallon. I thought how could you ever count that out, I'm never going to be able to learn the money. My cousin taught me the currency the next day, it was a lot easier than pounds, shillings and pence.

I had this image of America, big sky scrapers, huge department stores, beautiful women shopping in fur coats with lots of gift wrapped presents, luxury cars, mansions, fancy restaurants, money flowing like honey, the streets lined with gold, everything you could ever dream of but that was Hollywood I saw on the big screen and I had landed in NJ. Believe me NJ didn't disappoint me. I remember looking around a department store and seeing the crowds of people and I didn't know a single soul. I longed for someone to call out my name, Olive, Katherine, Irish, stupid, anything. I missed not seeing any familiar faces, everyone was a stranger. The house auntie Winnie worked in was a big mansion with a finished basement, I'd never even seen a basement before. It was situated on a tree lined street. I even had my own bedroom and bathroom. The old doctor was very welcoming and extremely thrifty. When he realized I could use a sewing machine he had me patching sheets even though he had brand new sets in the linen closet. He studied the supermarket sales fliers and stocked up on sale items. That was another first, the huge supermarkets loaded with food I'd never even seen before let alone eat.

I balanced his books and his charitable contributions to the last penny for tax purposes. He was surprised I was so polite and courteous, he asked me if I always did everything auntie Winnie told me, of course I did, it's called respecting your elders.

Everything was fascinating about America. It was freezing outside but you came into a nice warm building. It seemed the temperature inside was the same all year round, no draughts, no chills, no hatching the fire getting chilblains. I came home freezing one day and started looking for the fire, I thought how do people warm themselves without cozying up to a fire, they had central heating that's how, even the cars were heated. The popular songs were "I got you babe" by Sonny & Cher, "Downtown" by Petula Clark and the Beatles had just arrived before me. We'd been listening to the Beatles for years back home, I didn't know what the big hullabaloo was all about. I didn't much care for their crazy music besides that they were from England and at that time there was no love lost between the Irish and the English because of how they treated us in the past. The popular shows were Lawrence Welk Saturday nights and Ed Sullivan Sunday nights. My sister Mary asked me to get little Joe's autograph from Little House on the Prairie, or Elvis, like I was going to bump into them on the street. Daddy gave me a list of people from home who had relatives in America and wanted me to look them up. They stretched from New York to California. Sure, no problem, I'll check them all out next week.

My First Job In America

Auntie Winnie came with me when I interviewed at the telephone company and the bank. The telephone company accepted me but they said I'd have to go to school for 6 weeks, that's all I needed to hear besides I hated telephone work. I'd never been to school in America and I didn't know what to expect, what if everyone was smarter than me, so I ended up taking a job at a bank. I took an entrance test and the personnel director said I got the highest score she'd ever seen in spelling. I didn't think I passed because there were words like "jewelry" vs. "jewellery" I'd never seen these words abbreviated before. One up for the nuns, they were very strict about math and spelling. Just one thing she said "if you're going to use your pet name Olive, you will have to use your legal name Katherine whenever you sign a legal document". How was I to know a legal document from a hole in the wall so I told her I'd stick with Katherine. I hardly knew myself anymore, new name, new country, no family, no friends. I felt like little red riding hood lost in the woods.

I was working the third day I came to America. On my first morning Auntie Winnie took me to the bus stop and told the driver to let me off on First St. I sat back and enjoyed the ride in the beautiful snow all snuggled up in my new suede jacket. People were getting off the bus at different stops until there was only me and the driver left. He looked in the mirror and said "where do you get off young lady". I said First St. He said we'd long passed it but he was going to the depot and he'd drop me off on his way back into town. I was hours late for work on my first day but it didn't seem to matter, they were all taken in by the brogue. Then I realized I'd left my purse on the bus so auntie Winnie had to arrange to retrieve it. I wasn't used to carrying a purse. After the first day I learned granny was mistaken about the banks closing at 2 o'clock, they were just closing the teller window, we still had to work until five.

The work was so easy you could do it blindfolded but I'd never worked in a production environment before so I set out to be the highest producer and I soon became the champ. I thought if people worked this hard in Ireland they'd be millionaires, back home we spent Monday mornings sitting on our desks discussing the dance the night before. Also, I noticed it was all work and no play except on weekends. Back home the day just began when we got home from work and we stayed up 'til all hours ceiliing. We'd send out for fish and chips at 11pm. now it's Chinese. With daylight savings it was still light at 10pm and dark when we went to work at 8am so we stayed up late and slept late. Another thing I noticed was that work was very informal. People were calling their boss by their first name. Back home it was Mr. or Mrs. That part I loved because it made them less intimidating.

When I got my first paycheck I thought I was an instant millionaire, I went from making $4.50 a week to $36. I sent money home every payday. I thought we'd be millionaires by the time I went back. That was the reason I came here in the first place. It seemed all my co-workers had Irish roots but nobody knew what part of Ireland they came from. I made a promise there and then if I ever had kids in this country they were going to know where I came from and they do. And they'll know everything about me when they read this book. It seemed nobody was a real American, they were French, German, Polish, Italian American or whatever, it was a melting pot for the world. Wasn't anybody just American, back home everyone was just Irish. Of course that's all changed now since Ireland joined the European Union (EU). I don't understand all this fuss about color, life would be boring if we all looked the same. I didn't want to stick out like a sore thumb so I tried to fit in and lost my identity over the years in a world of political correctness. I should have valued my Irishness but there were no other Irish people around so I just tried to fit in. People didn't understand my colloquialisms and it wasn't worth having to explain myself all the time so I dropped the slang and spoke like they did. One time I answered with a "pardon" and they made fun of me. A co -worker even commented on how I ate a banana, peeling it as I ate it, she said the proper way was to peel the whole banana at one time. I was embarrassed, I had so much to learn. The song "Mammy" by Al Jolson was very popular so I started referring to my mammy as my mother in case people would make fun of me. I ate everything with a knife and fork just like I'd been taught, here they were eating French fries with their hands, no manners! Ordering breakfast was an experience:

How do you want your eggs? cooked of course,

Did I want them over easy, hard, fried, poached?

What's over easy?

Toast, what kind? What do you mean?

Did I want white, rye, wheat, bagel, English muffin?

I don't eat anything English.

How do you want your steak? rare, medium rare or well done?

huh! you gotta be kidding me, which is pink in the middle?

Tea, now what can be complicated about a cup of tea,

Did I want it hot, cold, regular, decaf, green, black?

Oh no! At home we only drank hot black tea.

Cream or sugar? Of course, who takes tea without cream and sugar.

Milk or half and half?

Why was everything so complicated. I would hate to be a waitress here.

My First Shopping Spree

Auntie Winnie took me shopping for clothes. Then she made me pretend I brought them from Ireland. My co-workers commented on how the Irish dressed so much like the Americans, yea right! Then we went to the drug store to get something to hide my rosy cheeks. The lady told my aunt "they pay to have cheeks like that in America". Then there was the deodorant, we didn't have that at home and I never sweated until I started using it and God forbid you wore the same clothes two days in a row, you must be kidding me, I often wore the same clothes for a week, and a bath every day instead of weekly. Maybe my father was right, he claimed Americans were pale because their blood was all dried up from taking too many hot baths.

I loved all the luxuries in America, women had it much easier here. You could be doing laundry in your automatic washing machine, cleaning your self cleaning oven, running your dishwasher and vacuuming all at the same time. How my mother would have loved that and you hardly ever had to iron anything thanks to permanent press material. In spite of all that I was terribly homesick, I cried myself to sleep every night, I slept on a wet pillow. I didn't tell Auntie Winnie because I knew she was homesick too. The next day I was half dead from lack of sleep, then I saw a commercial for Geritol. They claimed it gave you energy. I started taking it and I could jump over a roof I had so much energy for the first few hours and then I collapsed. Someone told me it was full of alcohol and that was why it gave you a sudden spurt of energy so my being a pioneer I gave it up.

Life Can Be Lonely Even In This Big Country

I missed my family so much, especially my Mother and Regina. I remember thinking when I go back I'm going to hug my Mother so hard I'm never going to let go. And no more shaking hands with daddy, I was going to give him a big bear hug. Then a country and western song came out "my mother got run over by a reindeer". That night I dreamt I was getting off the plane and my mother ran out on the tarmac to meet me and she got run over by a baggage carrier. The only consolation was that I was just here until I got rich and then I was going back home. Fifty six years later I'm still here, I must never have reached my goal. I would never have come if I thought I was here to stay, I was too close to my family to leave them for good. I was just here to make mammy's life easier and I was going back as soon as I made that first million. My friend wrote and said she met my mother downtown and when she asked about me she started crying. Now I knew my mother's heart was breaking too which made things worse. I was the oldest girl and my mother was my best friend. Auntie Winnie was like a second mother to me. She was so good. Remember I'd known her for years before she came to America. She now had a boyfriend, the first I ever remember her having. He was from the west coast of Ireland. A big heavy set guy. Fond of the bottle, his drink was a beer and a shot. Auntie Winnie was a pioneer just like myself. That's a pledge you take at confirmation never to drink.

They were both very active in an Irish American group who promoted the Irish culture in America. I went to all their meetings and dances, the youngest by about 40 years. They used to gather around a piano singing that's when I realized daddy had made up his own words to the Irish songs. I felt I had left behind the best years of my life. In Ireland we had top show bands, crowded dancehalls and here I was underage, unable to go anywhere because alcohol was served and I was under 21. I also noticed people throwing darts at a JFK dartboard. I was shocked, the Irish at home loved JFK and were broken hearted when he was assassinated. We loved him because he was an Irish Catholic we had no idea what his politics were. I wasn't interested in politics, I hardly knew who the President of Ireland was. Another thing, I was horrified the way the media criticized their president. It was like Catholics criticizing the pope. Whatever happened to respecting your leader, we would never dream of doing that in Ireland at that time but now that's changed. You don't have to like him but at least respect the office.

Auntie Winnie and friends stayed out all Saturday night after a dance. We had breakfast in a diner (a new experience) and we slept in the car in the church parking lot so we could go to early mass Sunday morning and then go home and sleep 'til noon. It was so much fun, a lot different from sneaking into grannies at 3am. One time we went to the Monaghan ball in NY. I recognized a guy who'd skipped town after getting a girl pregnant. Another time we went to wrestling in Madison Square Garden and later to the taping of an Oprah show.

Well life went on and soon I met an Irish American guy at the Irish Club. He called me Olivia, I guess it sounded royal or something. The poor guy couldn't dance, when he did the twist everyone around him got kicked. That didn't last long because dancing was very important to me although I thought the music wouldn't hold a candle to the Irish show bands. Remember the pen, well this guy wanted me to touch his pen the first time we went to a drive in movie. No way, the only weenies I'd ever touched was my baby brothers when I gave them a bath. What's this obsession with weenies anyway! Doesn't anyone just kiss any more? The World's Fair was in NY so he and I went with an organization that was sponsoring a group of underprivileged kids. These kids were sex crazy, they chased after the opposite sex all over the fair, we could hardly keep track of them. They were whistling at girls out of the bus, I wanted to die. I hardly saw anything at the fair because we were so busy chasing after them. He also introduced me to my first fast food drive in, just like I'd seen in the movies and lobster which I thought was gross.

Auntie Winnie and I were at the bus stop on our way to visiting her friends in Elizabeth city when a young guy pulled up in a car and asked if we wanted a ride. We got in, can you imagine doing that today. He was Italian, a guinea, as auntie Winnie called him with a last name I couldn't even begin to pronounce let alone spell. This was my first Italian acquaintance and he never stopped talking the whole way to Elizabeth. Auntie Winnie said he must have been injected with a gramophone needle. She was very witty. The friends we were visiting were from home, they had a son in Vietnam and were anxiously awaiting a call from him. They passed the phone around to everyone, they were so excited to hear his voice. He made it home safely thank God. The houses were so close they could shout out their kitchen window to the neighbor.

My First Bathroom Experience

Another friend of auntie Winnies was grand Marshall of the St. Patrick's Day parade in Newark so I was right up front. I had to come to America to march in my first St. Patrick's day parade, imagine! Everyone was wearing green including myself. It was freezing cold and I had a suit on. My fingers were so cold, I thought I had frost bite. As soon as we arrived at the Irish restaurant in Newark I ran into the bathroom to run warm water on my fingers to thaw them out. When I came out there was a line of men waiting to use the bathroom. I apologized but one man said it's okay but do you know you were in the men's bathroom. I had no idea women and men had separate bathrooms, what a luxury! Actually I was a bit curious how people sat on those weird toilets (urinals) and I didn't like the fact that you did it out in the open. I thought of Gerard and the community showers. I goofed up one more time at a drive in theater. I went in one side of the big screen to use the bathroom and the men went in the other and we met in the middle. Then there was the St. Patrick's Day tradition of corn beef and cabbage. I'd never had it before in my life, who said that was an Irish dish? It's like saying Pizza is the national dish of Italy.

My first American bath was an experience. I filled the tub with boiling hot water first and when I went back the bathroom was filled with steam, I had to open a window and stick my head out to breathe. Everyone seemed to be drinking beer so I tried it and thought it was awful, still don't like it. I was amazed at all the drinking that went on in American homes and they had the nerve to accuse the Irish of being drunks. The only drink you got in an Irish home was a cup of tea, you had to go to the pub to get alcohol. I chased my first squirrel down the road to get a picture to send home to Regina. I never saw a squirrel in Ireland. I felt all alone in this country except for auntie Winnie. Millions of people and I didn't know a soul. I thought if I died in this country there'd be no one at my funeral. I remember following a guy on the street that looked a bit Irish but when he spoke he said howdy so I knew he was no Irishman. I guess the cowboy hat and the boots should have been a clue. I missed people running in and out of the house. Here you had to be invited.

Work And Those Almighty Dollars

Work was going good, I was moving up, I got promoted to another department. The girls were nice although I thought they were very immature and I noticed they had big thick thighs, maybe because they didn't have to walk like we did, they went from the house to the car. The work was a no brainer. The money kept coming in and auntie Winnie wouldn't take any money from me, she'd rather I send it home, everything was going according to plan. I would be a millionaire in no time and I could return home. I had teenage zits so one of my co-workers pointed out a girl with pot holes in her face. She said it used to be a lot worse before she brought her to a cosmetic studio. I couldn't imagine but I didn't want that to happen to me so I went along. They gave me a facial, I looked like I was going to perform on Broadway. I bought the whole treatment, a face mask and foundation cream which they claimed you didn't have to wash off at night, it kept on working.

That suited me. It worked, but I was almost 19 so my face would probably have cleared up soon anyway. I remained loyal to this studio for years, even brought my girls to it when they went through their teenage zit years. I got warts for the first time in my life so my mother sent me out wart remover, Gypsy gold panty hose and boiled Christmas pudding in a can. It lasted so long it went blue molded.

One day I met the VP of the bank on the elevator. He asked me if I was going to the annual company picnic. That's when I first got introduced to corn on the cob, we used to give it to the pigs, I didn't know you could eat it or how. I started to eat it with a knife and fork until I saw people looking at me funny. Then I watched them pick it up in their hands. Then came square dancing which was our version of country and western dancing. I thought the Irish must have brought it over here and they copied it. I was a pro at that, remember dancing was my thing. I even danced with the old VP. I started playing checkers on our lunch break and soon earned the title of champion. The word got out and the VP challenged me to a game. Everyone in the department was there for the showdown. I had very strict rules, if you moved a draft out of it's square and you took your finger off, you couldn't put it back. Fair enough right! Well needless to say, the VP wasn't willing to play by the rules so I was beaten in the first round. Who was I to argue with the VP of the bank I was working in, I'm not that stupid. I just let him have his day in the sun. It was nice having the title while it lasted.

I wrote home to mammy telling her Americans ate different than us, they ate fruit with their dinner, i.e. applesauce with pork and cranberry sauce with chicken, weird! And they drank with their meals. We had our tea after we ate. Maybe it wasn't such a bad idea, it washed the food down. I never heard of mayonnaise and I didn't like it so I ate tuna fish right out of the can on buttered bread. There had to be butter on everything. And all these big long names like Mangione, Bernardo, Rodriguez, no Irish names there although I wished my name was Moriarity instead of Clarke. I felt if I ever lost my accent I'd never be able to prove I was Irish.

There's a First Time For Everything

I'll never forget the first day I left work and headed into the steaming hot humidity, I thought I stuck my head in an oven. I could hardly breathe, I was suffocating. How could anyone survive in this but like everything else you get used to it. I'd rather have the cold any day though. Summer is my least favorite time of year. One time I went to a college campus with some of the girls from work. They stopped for pizza, I'd never seen pizza before, it looked like someone had thrown up on a piece of dough. I could have puked, I love it today though. The campus was a scary experience, guys sitting on porches calling girls inside, drinking beer, loud music. I didn't drink and I started noticing some of my friends had disappeared. Nobody seemed concerned. I was petrified, I thought I'd never get out of there alive. I never went back. Later on I found out we were at a frat party. I accidentally slammed the car door on my finger coming home and ended up in the ER. An English doctor took care of me and he said "give me an English trained nurse any day". It seems they had more hands on experience.

My neighbors invited me to a dance at a country club, that's where they had met and married so they thought it might be lucky for me. And that's when I met Charlie Jones, all these big Italian names and I meet a Charlie Jones, the most common name in Ireland. It was love at first sight, the skinny teddy boy type with dark curly hair slicked back. I didn't know it then but he was 17 years my senior and had been divorced with a kid. We were already too far into the relationship when I found out. He had a brother marrying an Irish girl and he said "wouldn't my mother love to have 2 Irish girls in the family". I thought this is a fast worker. I met his family the next weekend and was invited to the wedding. The bride to be, Veronica was from the north of Ireland and we hit it off right away. I stayed weekends down the shore with them.

Eventually Charlie and I did the unthinkable, we committed mortal sin, but only when I felt sure he loved me enough to marry me, now I was emotionally involved. I had this belief, kiss me and I'm in love, go to bed with me and you're stuck with me forever. I was ashamed of myself but this was an experienced guy and I didn't want to lose him. So I gave him what he wanted and I stressed out about getting pregnant and having to tell it in confession because auntie Winnie would be suspicious if I didn't go to Holy Communion. I was desperate for someone to love me, I wanted to belong to someone, anyone.

I cried every time I wrote home, always pretending I was happy. One time I broke down and wrote my mother that my heart was breaking and I wasn't happy here. The ink was running from my tears and then I thought if I don't go back this will break her heart so I tore it up and wrote the usual "everything's great" letter. Besides I was in love and no longer a virgin so I had to marry Charlie Jones, no one else would want me. I'd broken all the rules, he was divorced, an atheist only 3 years younger than my father and we were behaving like a married couple. See what happens when you let your kids loose.

Halloween in America was a lot different than back home. They got treats, we just got angry neighbors. Here it was heaven, getting dressed up, getting enough candy to last all year, rotting our teeth etc. Christmas was rolling around, I was 11 months in America. My heart was breaking for my family, I couldn't stay away any longer. I made up my mind to go home on an open ticket. The bank suggested I take a six week leave of absence but I turned it down because I had no idea if I'd ever come back but then I had that Charlie thing and that mortal sin hanging over my head. I told him I was just going home for Christmas. I got busy shopping and bought presents for everyone, I got engraved watches for mammy and daddy. I got every size and shape of Levi jeans and would you believe there was a pair to fit everyone. I got daddy undershorts because men didn't wear them at home at that time. My aunt dared him to go outside in them, she thought they were for wearing outside. They had a shine on the back of their trousers. I even got one of those screens you adjust to fit the window so I wouldn't get eaten alive in bed with flies and wasps, I also brought fitted sheets which I thought my mother would love but they were cotton and I'd forgotten it's so cold over there in Winter they needed flannel sheets to keep them warm.

GOING BACK HOME AND ALL THE CHANGES

The day finally came and I was so happy to be back home, it was like I had been given a second chance. As we landed at Shannon I was in awe at the countryside, it was like a patchwork quilt with all the different shades of green fields. No wonder Johnny Cash was inspired to write "the 40 shades of green" when he first saw it. Sometimes we don't see the beauty all around us until we lose it. Mammy looked the same, she always looked her best, hair done, makeup on. Regina and the rest had grown a little. I later learned she had become the official pick pocket of the family. It was now her turn to "steal" money out of daddy's trouser's pocket when he fell asleep drunk. By now he had enough money to separate the different denominations into separate rolls and she'd take a few notes out of each roll so he wouldn't notice. I used to just go straight for the big ones and run. I wonder if he ever caught on to us. We all did it over the years but it was for a good cause. Recently I did it to my husband and he woke up and just said "hi, honey". He trusted me, he knew I wasn't robbing him. Michael had gotten chubby but after a month on a cousin's farm in the north he came back skinny. The last 4 in our family were smoking like trains, what happened, wasn't anyone afraid of daddy anymore. He did seem to have mellowed a little. Remember that uninhabitable bedroom, well it was all fixed up now with American dollars, the castle was next. Everything looked smaller, the house, the streets, the church, even that long walk to the post office was just a skip and a jump away, you walked farther in a department store in America. The roads looked like lanes compared to American highways and everyone had cars. What happened, I was only gone 11 months, did everyone win the lottery. It still rained every day but that was a blessing compared to the humidity of the American summers. There were new housing developments, strangers living in our town and Bose radio had opened a plant there. How could all this happen in just eleven months. Tom was now running the church choir. I'd hate to see what would happen if I'd stayed away longer. Children were actually skipping and laughing coming and going to school. Something's not right, had all the nuns died? I visited the convent and told my last teacher there that every time I dreamt about school it was a nightmare. She seemed shocked. She later had a nervous breakdown and left the convent. I don't think it was anything I said, I don't think they realized how much we feared them, what a shame because we got a good education. I went to see my old coworkers and my boss offered me my job back with a raise. He offered me £7 a week, about $20 but I had to promise not to tell anyone, I would be the highest paid on the staff. I was making way more than that in America but I was so happy to be back with my family I accepted. I often wondered if my mother or granny were disappointed in me. I had the chance of a lifetime going to America and I blew it. I went back to work, I didn't tell Charlie.

The troubles in the north had broken out by then and whenever we crossed the border into the north we would see devastation. A house was blown up because the woman gave tea to the British soldiers. An abandoned bus was on the side of the road and nobody would touch it because it could be rigged to blow up. Women were tarred and feathered for associating with British soldiers and an Irishman on his way home from church was murdered and left on his mother's doorstep with his penis in his mouth. Then a young British soldier who was flirting with the school girls was found strangled by the panels on a wrought iron fence around the church. One time Tom was held captive crossing the border going to work in Newry and his car stolen and a bomb placed in it outside of a store. This was the work of the British and the IRA, an illegal Irish republican army. It was tit for tat, an eye for an eye.

Another time daddy, Irene and I went to a family funeral in the north. They had to take the coffin out their living room window because they couldn't turn it to get it out the front door. As we were walking in the funeral procession to the church a soldier mingled with the crowd. This was how they safely got from point A to point B. Auntie Minnie walked us to the house and told us not to be scared if we heard a noise behind a wall that it was just soldiers and they wouldn't touch us. Yea right! We were making tea at her house and when we were rinsing the tea leaves out of the pot and throwing them out the back we heard a noise, nothing to worry about, just a soldier with a rifle pointed at us, no sweat! We always had a sing song when we visited her and one time we ended the night singing the Irish national anthem. You gotta be kiddin me, we were surrounded by British soldiers, that was really pushing our luck.

Auntie Minnie lived alone after granny died and even though she was blind she was quite self-sufficient. I always regretted not sitting down with her and documenting our family history. She had a great memory. Remember that funeral we went to? Well daddy spent the whole evening in a pub and was feeling no pain by the end of the day and to top it off he was our designated driver, lucky us! He was driving all over the road, we prayed all the way home. If you've never been to Ireland you'd think the man was drunk that engineered the roads, you'd get dizzy driving on them they wind and wind and no traffic lights and the people drive like maniacs. Irene whispered to me, can you drive a car if you have to, no, not a stick shift. Actually to this day I've never even tried a stick or driven in Ireland. In hindsight we would have been safer jerking than swerving. I don't know how we came off safe, our guardian angel was watching over us.

Charlie came home to get me after 3 weeks but I wasn't ready. I couldn't leave my family, not just yet, I needed more time. I never told my family he was atheist or divorced, daddy would have killed me. He pretended to go to mass but went for a walk out the road and arrived back with the crowd from mass, no one was any the wiser. Daddy took him down to the pub and they gave him some poitin (moonshine). Daddy always said you couldn't trust a man that didn't drink.

He went back to America without me and we wrote for 9 months, sometimes 2 letters a day. His first letter would say "I miss you, I love you" and the next "if you don't come back soon I'm going to find someone else, there's plenty of girls in America". I was very torn because I wanted to be home with my family but I missed him terribly and I knew I had to marry him otherwise I never would have "done it" and besides no one else would want me now that I was used goods. The old saying is true, you can never go back, nothing is the same even after only eleven months. A whole new generation of kids had grown up and were taking over our territory. The guys that chased us were now chasing them. I was almost 20 now. In those days if you weren't spoken for by 20 you were destined to be an old maid. A guy asked me if all girls in America put out because a girl from our town had been to America and now she was easy play for all the guys. He was one of her customers but then he had the nerve to say if he ever married a girl and discovered on his wedding night that she wasn't a virgin, he would kick her out of the bed. Now I knew for sure I had to marry Charlie. You see the double standard, it was okay for the men to play but they would only marry a virgin.

One time a neighbor told us daddy's horses got out of the field and were running down the hill. I went down to the pub to get him, his home away from home. He introduced me to his friends, some I knew, and asked me to blow (treat) everyone to a drink. I told him I had no money with me that I just came down to tell him about the horses. He said "I never saw a bloody yank that ever had a penny or would put their hand in their pocket". Every American was a yank and they had the reputation of being tight with money, although the Irish wouldn't let them pay for a drink anyway, they'd rather show off.

In August I went on summer vacation to Irene in Wexford when I got word that Charlie was back in town. It came through the police station. That's how they communicated if you didn't have a phone. I went back home knowing this was it, if I didn't go back with him this time it was over. But I also knew if I did go back it would be for good. I couldn't quite read Mammy, I didn't know if she wanted me to go or not but

I guess she left it up to me. We "did it" while Charlie was home and now I had to tell it to an Irish priest in confession. I disguised my voice and the priest gave me absolution saying, "that was when you were in America right". I wanted to die, he recognized my voice. To this day I only go to confession to visiting priests.

Do I Have To Go Back?

The night before I left for America I sat looking out the window at all the familiar faces and places and realized I was no longer going to be a part of it all. I don't know if I could have settled at home any more after experiencing all the luxuries of America. What you never had you never miss but once you get a taste of the good life it's hard to go back. I couldn't take hanging out clothes on a line, hatching the fire to keep warm, carrying buckets of hot water, rain all year round, the dampness, the hard times etc. Of course that is no longer. I loved the four seasons in America, back home you couldn't tell one season from the other. The only bad part was I had to give up my family. It was harder leaving this time because I knew it would be for good. Charlie and I planned on getting married. There goes my dream of living up the street from mammy and stopping by with my kids. From now on I would be the visitor from America. I wouldn't see my siblings grow up or be a part of their everyday lives. And who was going to watch over them and keep them away from the perverts. They could get away with murder with mammy, she was so naive. I was so protective of them, more like a spy, they used to say how long more until you go back to America.

Back To America for Good

I went back to America with Charlie and still no band to greet me, they still didn't get the memo. Regina was now 10, still a young kid and I knew she'd be growing up without me, I was broken hearted. Who was going to protect and guide her. If I could have taken her with me I would. I lived with auntie Winnie and got a job in a supermarket in the meat department because I knew it was only temporary, I only stayed a week. I didn't know one piece of meat from the other, it was all just meat to me. A customer rang the bell and asked for a porterhouse steak. I thought he knew I was Irish and was just fooling me, porter, stout. I was on the register another day but I'd never made change in U.S. currency in my life so I counted the change in pennies, I didn't know how to do it in increments. People thought it was cute because of the brogue but I was frustrated as hell. We had a price list for produce but that wasn't much help if you didn't recognize what it was. I'd have to ask them what do you call that. I left without collecting my pay check, that was not my cup of tea. I worked for another week in a factory on a production line folding towels. I was no speedy Gonzalez there either, a physically challenged girl who trained me was more productive. Needless to say I left there before payday. I didn't want a job with training involved because I was just killing time waiting on our marriage license.

Within a month we were married by a justice of the peace, no family, just his brother Al and Veronica as witnesses. The mayor who married us was named Charlie Jones and running for re-election so it made the local papers "Charlie Jones marries Charlie Jones". So much for keeping secrets. We shopped at the mall for a wedding ring. It was not the wedding most people dream of. I wouldn't have wanted a big splash anyway without my family, and I wasn't exactly a virgin bride. Charlie took religious instructions from an Irish priest but he told me to go ahead and marry outside the church because he didn't think the marriage would last and I'd be free to marry again. I got a bank job in Trenton, it was easy because I had the experience. I took 2 buses to work every day and then Charlie picked me up in Wrightstown. There were young military guys everywhere, it was during the Vietnam war. We lived in a mobile home, it was new and compact, very nice although I'd never lived in one before. I don't think that was the American dream my mother had in mind. Back home only Gypsies lived in those so I never told her. There were lots of trailer parks around because we lived by the army base and Charlie worked at the Air Force base as a civilian. When he first told me he worked for the government I thought he worked in the White House.

An Irish friend gave me a book of Irish sweepstakes tickets to sell which Charlie sold at the base. I didn't know my coworkers well enough for them to trust me. The agreement was the seller got one free ticket in the book and the person taking the risk got the other one because they were illegal to sell in America. Well, as luck would have it Charlie won 3rd prize but he and his friends used the same nom de plume and his friends put in a claim saying they agreed to split the winnings 3 ways. All 3rd party claims must be settled in the Irish courts before the winnings will be released. It took 2 years of going back and forth with a local Irish lawyer before it was settled. I didn't mind because I loved to go home. Charlie agreed to split the winnings 3 ways because this case would get a lot of publicity in the media over there and I was afraid his family history would be revealed and my family would be humiliated so for their sake he settled out of court. They each got $9k after all legal expenses.

As luck would have it, the English estate owner who owned most of the houses on our street was putting them up for sale. Up to that point people paid the rates (taxes) on the house which was collected by a local solicitor but when he died nobody replaced him and everyone got away scot free for years. Daddy put $2500 down as a deposit on our house with a receipt showing a balance owing of $7k. He kept that receipt folded in his breast pocket for over 40 years, it was tearing at the folds. When he died Tom was able to purchase the house for the $7k. They were selling for $80k by then but the receipt was a legal document and they had to honor it. What a stroke of luck!

Mary Comes To America

Following a miscarriage I had a successful pregnancy but it was company policy to go out on maternity leave at 5 months. I was throwing up day and night, I used to have to stop the bus on the way to work to throw up. It was lonely living in the country with Charlie gone all day so I wrote home and asked if anyone would like to come to America. Mary took me up on the offer. A few months later she arrived, all 95 lbs. of her with hair down to her waist and mini skirts and maxi coats. She was beautiful.

By now we had a house but it was a handy man special and my handyman was MIA. We bought all our furniture in Philly at an auction, it was slightly smoke damaged from the fires during the racial riots. I bought reams of material and made all our curtains. Charlie taught me to use the washer and dryer at the laundromat, I had to write down the instructions. His first breakfast he asked me for a 2 minute boiled egg. Sounds easy enough right, except I didn't know when to start timing it, as soon as I turned the knob? do I use cold or hot water? He got me an egg timer but that didn't help, I didn't know when to flip it. After a few days and a few hard boiled eggs against the wall I figured it out. An Italian lady at work wrote down the recipe for spaghetti and meatballs. She forgot the water, I didn't know what it was supposed to look like, I'd never seen it before, but when Charlie asked where's the sauce I knew something was wrong it was all dried up. I had a few more goof ups. I was dying for sausages for breakfast so I bought these great big sausages and cooked them for breakfast. I found out they were hot dogs. One time I bought what I thought was the red salmon we had on Fridays back home. The butcher went to slice it real thin and I told him I wanted it thick. I floured and fried it and it was tough as nails. I later found out it was lox. I was hopeless, Mammy was a great mother but she didn't prepare us for marriage. Charlie taught me to cook and from then on he never set foot in the kitchen.

Welcome Coleen

Coleen, my oldest was born Nov. 4th, 1968, the day Nixon was elected president. She weighed 9 lbs.11 oz. at birth with red hair, thank God it later turned blonde. She was the largest baby in the nursery. There was a scout from a disposable diaper company looking for a baby to put on their diaper boxes, I was sure he'd pick Coleen but he didn't. She never looked like a newborn, she looked like a three month old, maybe that's why she didn't get the job. There was no pay, just the privilege of having your baby on the diaper box. When I came home from the hospital Veronica and her family were there and I had to sit on the toilet in the bathroom to breast feed my brand new baby because I couldn't climb the stairs.

Coleen never knew what it was to go to bed awake she always slept on Mary's shoulder or her daddy's stomach. I tried breastfeeding her but she was always hungry, so the doctor changed her to formula. That didn't agree with her either so Charlie prepared regular milk with Karo syrup and she did great, he put a small pillow in her crib and she slept through the night. She was spoiled rotten and never had any reason to cry, she was so pampered. We'd peek into her crib and watch her sleep hoping she'd wake soon. Mary and I watched soaps while she napped, General Hospital, Days of our lives etc.

Mary lived with us for six months babysitting a little military kid. It was so nice having her around but I knew it was no life for her. One time she went to the bank to cash her check but it was closed. She walked up to the drive-in window and they told her she'd have to get in line so she got behind the last car breathing in the fumes and waited her turn. She got a notice from the dept. of immigration telling her she had to leave the country within 30 days. She got an extension of 6 months but then got a final notice to be out of the country by xx date. She didn't want to go back. By now I was married to an American citizen 3 years and eligible to become an American citizen. I was concerned when I took the oath to take up arms against my native country in wartime but I said to myself "no way" and hoped I would never be put to the test. They didn't have dual citizenship then. I claimed Mary and now she was a legal alien. That was the legal process to enter this country not crossing the border illegally like they do now. Mary moved to Westfield, stayed with auntie Winnie, got a job and later married an Irish man from Belfast.

Back To Ireland

We went back to Ireland when Coleen was about 10 months old. She cried the whole flight because she didn't want to sleep in the little cardboard baby bed they provided and she was cutting teeth. She cut her first teeth in Ireland and wouldn't you know it they later turned out to be big buck teeth. She had to wear braces for 3 years. My mother was amazed at the comparison between her and a baby of the same age that she babysat. Coleen was drinking out of a glass (no sippy cups then) and eating baby food with a spoon. The other poor kid was still on the bottle and could barely sit up he was so chubby. Mammy assumed American babies were smarter. There was no baby food at home then so they chewed the food in their mouth before giving it to the baby. Yuck! They wet the pacifier in their mouth and then stuck it in the sugar bowl. Great way to introduce them to sugar. I was making oatmeal for Coleen one morning and daddy asked for some. It was instant, he said it tasted like the shavings from the barn. Coleen was playing house and she asked daddy if he wanted to go to McDonalds. At that time they hadn't hit Ireland yet so daddy thought she was talking about a person and said no, not today but tell Mrs. McDonald I said hello. Coleen slept in a crib in mammy's room, I hardly had to do a thing, mammy tended to her every need. She said I had more trouble with one kid than she had with 8. She wanted me to leave Coleen there until we came back at Christmas for the sweepstake hearing. No way, I was not leaving without her.

Daddy was drinking more than ever. I begged mammy to come back with me and take Regina and Gerard, they were the only ones still living at home. She said "if I had it to do all over again, I'd still marry him". God help her, she really loved him in spite of everything. Of course she was raised with the old saying "you made your bed, you lie in it". There was no such thing as divorce and if anyone got pregnant out of wedlock they could skip over to England and either have the baby and put it up for adoption or get an abortion and come back like nothing ever happened. The men skipped the country too rather than face up to their responsibility and there was no law to force them to pay child support. Auntie Winnie told me daddy didn't always have a drinking problem but he accidentally killed a man that was working for him while he was backing up his horse truck. He never got over it and he had to make amends to the family, the guy was their sole support. It was then that he started to drink. Sounds logical but I've heard other stories.

We're In Business

Back in America we bought a building that was about to be condemned from this old guy who would rather sell it to us than allow the city to knock it down for a much needed parking lot. Charlie did all the repairs himself, he was a wanna be handyman but never finished a job. It was a one horse town mostly occupied by the military because of its proximity to the army and navy base. Charlie quit his job at the navy base and with his pension we opened a luncheonette and a general merchandise store and leased the other store out for a beauty salon. We rented the three apartments upstairs to military people and moved into the biggest one. Coleen was two years old when we moved to the apartment. I remember she was only as high as the handle on the oven door. She looked around and said "I wike this house, did my daddy buy this house P me". The general merchandise we sold in our store was unclaimed merchandise auctioned off at the Philly docks. Charlie went to the auction every Tuesday, he bought, I sold. I never knew what he'd come home with. I was very naive at first in the store, I trusted everyone, I didn't know there were thieves everywhere. People brought clothes into the dressing room to try on and passed them out the back door to their partners in crime. Others would drive up to the back door for sheets of paneling and load up their truck and only pay for 10 sheets. I was alone in the store with the kids and I couldn't follow them around. Needless to say we were robbed blind. I never thought people could be so dishonest, it was an eye opener. One time Coleen was picking her nose in the doctor's office and the nurse told her that was not nice. She turned and said to her "then how do you get the buggers out of your nose".

Welcome Jennifer

We were pretty busy with the stores and I was pregnant again with Jennifer. She only weighed 6lbs. 8ozs. at birth, she was tiny and fragile compared to Coleen. She had a big mop of blonde curly hair at birth. People used to ask if she was wearing a wig. Charlie and Coleen came to pick us up at the hospital and Coleen accidentally stuck her finger in Jennifer's eye trying to hold her. Jen was a difficult baby to raise and she was allergic to disposable diapers, just my luck with no washing machine. One morning she was crying hysterically and Charlie got some coke from the store and put it in her bottle and she burped up loads of gas. We learned she was allergic to rice cereal. The pediatrician said he felt there was something wrong with her but he couldn't pin point it so he sent us for blood work. She went into fits so they were unable to complete it. Later we found out he was correct. She didn't like to be held, she'd squirm off my lap and she was stubborn as all hell. Whenever we went out in the car the three girls sat in the back seat, no car seats then. The other two jumped out when they were told but not Jen, I'd have to climb in and pull her out. I read Dr. Benjamin Spock and tried to do all the latest and greatest things according to the expert, maybe the Irish way wasn't the only way. Some of it went against the grain for me because I believed in a good slap on the butt when they needed it, none of this psychology B.S. The pacifier was a blessing but then they said they'd get buck teeth from it. As it turns out 2 out of 3 needed braces so maybe they were right.

I took driving lessons from a driving school, failed the test the first time because I couldn't parallel park. Mary came with me the second time around. It was the wrong day but the right time so they took me. I was 8 months pregnant with my belly hitting the steering wheel. The Vietnam war was on and I think the inspector may have thought my husband was overseas and I might have to drive myself to the hospital in the middle of the night so he passed me. I bought Mary's old car and I was now self sufficient. The first time I drove there was a car illegally parked on a corner and I had to stop short. One of the kids hit the windshield (no seat belts). Our dog was in heat and she jumped out the window and all the dogs in the neighborhood chased after her. When I caught up with her and tried to put her back in the car the other dogs jumped in too. The kids were screaming.

Welcome Michele

Then came Michele on Coleen's birthday weighing 8lbs 9ozs. They were 3 years and 3 minutes apart. She was a good healthy baby, practically bald, we had to put bows on her few strands to show she was a little girl. She was no trouble at all, I was an old pro by now with instant formula and no sterilizing bottles. I remember when they called Charlie to tell him he had a baby girl, he said " not another girl". We never did have a boy, I never really wanted one, I joked that I didn't know how to potty train a boy, also we had the draft then and the Vietnam war was on. I didn't want to raise a boy to be sent to war. Besides that mammy used to say one boy was more trouble than the five girls put together. When I came home from the hospital with Michele our apartment was a disaster. I had asked Charlie to bring me an outfit to wear home and he must've thrown everything in the closet on the floor to find it. The curtains and curtain rods were on the floor, the box spring and mattress were on the floor, a stainless steel tea pot my mother had sent me was in the garbage with a hole burned out of it because he used it to boil eggs. In the children's room all the dresser drawers were pulled out and the clothes strewn all over the floor, some of them wet from the leaks in the ceiling. The phone rang, and it was Veronica inquiring when I was going to have my baby, he didn't even bother to tell his family I'd had Michele. I broke down and told her the condition of the apartment and she got in her car and came right down to help. While I was waiting I cleaned up as best I could, I was too embarrassed for anyone to see the condition of the place. I'm lucky I didn't hemorrhage putting the bed back together. When I complained to Charlie he told me he was too busy with the store while I lay resting in a hospital bed.

RAISING THE GIRLS, THE JOY OF MY LIFE

I had 3 girls by age 25, I was the oldest mother on the maternity floor with my last, not like today. I missed my mother so much, I would have given anything to have her close by, she would have loved the girls. I was raising the girls on my own. The girls were under 3 with 2 in cloth diapers and I had no washing machine so I ordered diaper service and went through 100 diapers a week. I'd pile up my laundry in pillowcases and put it in a stroller and walk to the laundromat with three small kids, I didn't have a car yet and Charlie wouldn't even drop us off. One night Veronica drank a bottle of wine while arguing with him about the lousy husband he was. He had a washer and dryer for sale in the store and wouldn't let me have it. Finally she talked him into giving it to me and I remember his words "as soon as she gets that she's going to want something else". The water pressure in the kitchen was so bad it took forever to fill the machine but it was a lot better than spending hours in the laundromat.

The girls grew up with Sesame Street, Captain Kangaroo and Mr. Rogers, then later I love Lucy, Little House on the Prairie and The Brady Bunch. Coleen was Marsha, Jen was Jan and Michele was Cindy. One time I sent Coleen to the drugstore up the street and the clerk said hi Coleen, she answered my name is Marsha. When they got older they promoted themselves to Charlie's Angels. One time a black lady came into our luncheonette and Coleen asked her if she was aunt Jemima. Coleen was always running away from home when I'd get mad at her. We had a guy working for us who used to tell her to wait until he got off work that he was running away too. She'd sit on a stool chatting up the customers while she waited for him. She packed a Mickey Mouse lunch box with a nightgown and a can of Campbell's chicken noodle soup. I stopped unpacking it because this was an everyday occurrence. When she'd come back upstairs she'd put her head in the door to make sure the coast was clear and say hello Mrs. Jones.

My life revolved around my girls. We played Barbies, house, school, sang nursery rhymes, watched cartoons, you name it we did it. I loved being a mom. Jennifer, took after my family for music, Michele, took after me for dancing, she had great rhythm, Coleen had neither voice nor rhythm, she was the teacher. I wanted these childhood years to last forever, I never wanted them to grow up and leave me like I did my mother.

We made up this song to the tune of "three little lassies from Banyon".

There were 3 little lassies from Pemberton, Pemberton, Pemberton, There were 3 little lassies from Pemberton,

Coleen, Jen & Michele were their names,

yea Coleen, Jen & Michele were their names.

Now these 3 little girls had a doggie, a doggie, a doggie,

now these 3 little girls had a doggie and Lady was her name,

Yea, Lady was her name".

Incidentally, lady was a white poodle that we got from one of our customers. She was loaded with fleas, we had to give her a flea bath and spend hours picking the fleas off her. She was Coleen's dog and one time we came home and she'd torn her pillow to shreds looking for her. whenever they were sick I'd buy them grapes. They thought they were so expensive we could only afford them when they were sick.

I opened up the luncheonette at 7a.m., ran upstairs at 9, got the kids dressed and fed, played with them for awhile and then put the two younger ones down for their nap from 11 to 1 and took Coleen with me back to the luncheonette for the lunch hour. I remember thinking I'd love to shake the hand of the man who invented cartoons because it kept them occupied while I was trying to get things done but as they got older and were pure heedless I wanted to kill him. Whenever I went down at night to check on things the luncheonette was usually full of teens, they had the pinball machines jammed so they could play free and the kid working for us had all his friends eating ice cream sundaes. All our help robbed us blind, we could never get the combination of an honest hard-working person so I had to spend a lot of time supervising them.

Married Life or Lack Of

Charlie was a loner, we very rarely did anything together. He felt it was a mother's job to raise girls and a fathers' to raise boys and since we didn't have any boys he was off the hook. Good cop out right!. He spent his weekends studying the racing form and going to the track. I went with him once before we had the girls. He'd spent the whole morning studying the racing form. I didn't know one horse from the other. I picked horses or jockeys with Irish names and won, he lost. Go figure! I don't know how to white wash my marriage but I'll be as kind as possible for the sake of my children. Charlie was a gambler but a decent provider, I never saw poverty nor did I ever see winnings. He gave me his paycheck to put in the bank and kept his winnings. I realized after a few months of marriage that I had made a big mistake. He was attentive while we were dating but once we were married he did his own thing. Maybe I expected too much. I expected him to fill the void left by my family and friends because I had left all of them for him. I had married for all the wrong reasons. He was a loner and should never have married but we got three beautiful girls out of the relationship and for that I will be forever grateful. Charlie was never home to notice what was going on, as long as there was gambling money in the register he was happy. He liked being the businessman but never wanted any of the responsibilities. One time we bought six little cabins. His intention was to fix them up and sell or rent them. Needless to say he did neither, we're lucky we got our money back out of them. He was a dreamer, always inventing things but you could buy the stuff at Home Depot.

Move Over America, Here Comes Michael!

About this time my mother wrote to me and asked if I would take Michael out. The troubles had started in Ireland and she was afraid he would get involved with the IRA. I hadn't seen him in years. He grew up tall and skinny and had a great personality. It was nice having him around, I could always count on him having my back. He always claimed he thought he was coming out to America on vacation but my mother only bought him a one way ticket.

I got some relief when he came because he kept an eye on things even if he helped himself, at least it stayed in the family. He worked in the luncheonette and cursed like a trooper at the school kids for taking so long to decide on a nickel piece of candy. Everyone loved him, including my kids. He told Jen she wasn't going to the same school as Coleen, that she was going to retarded school. She thought that was good news so she'd tell everyone in the store "guess what, my uncle Michael said I'm going to a special school, I'm going to betarded school". Sometimes I'd find his cowboy boots in the toy box where he'd thrown them at the girls because they were disturbing him. He was always teasing them sometimes to the point of tears but they loved him.

Once again he had an entourage of girls coming around and he treated them just like he did in Ireland, easy come easy go. One time an FBI agent came looking for him. I thought OMG what did he do now, we're all going to jail. It seems he bought and sold a watch that had been stolen out of a museum. He had to retrieve the watch and that was the last we saw of the FBI thank God. I swear if Al Capone had been around he would have been his right hand man though I don't think Michael would harm a soul. We used to say he'd steal the eye out of your head and come back for the eyebrow. He was a lot of hot air.

THE YANKEES ARE
COMING TO IRELAND!

Mammy was planning on coming out to visit but I didn't want her to see the conditions I was living in with buckets everywhere to catch the rain from the leaks in the roof. I wanted her to believe I was doing well in America. Then Granny got sick and was diagnosed with cancer. She lived another 10 years without any treatment or medication. Sometimes you have to wonder are we better off with or without the treatment. I went home with the girls to see her. That trip I only had to pay the airline taxes because kids under 3 flew free and I had 3 of them. Michele was a chubby baby and I had to carry her, with Coleen and Jen by my side, up and down escalators plus a bag of toys to keep them occupied. I had black and blue marks on my arms when I got home because sometimes I had to carry 2 kids because Jen kept taking off at the airport, I put her on a harness coming back. Every time I got them dressed to go for a walk it would rain. Hats off, coats off and the sun would come out. We did that a couple of times a day. That's typical of Irish weather. We stayed six weeks. That was the last time Coleen saw mammy.

Another time I went home with Jen 10, Michele 9 and their cousin Michael 6. Coleen couldn't come for some reason. I wrote home that I was coming but there was a bank holiday that weekend and we got home before the letter so there was no one to meet us at the airport. We took a bus to Reginas' but we were no sooner on it than there was a bomb scare and we had to get off. This was during the troubles. We then took a taxi but the driver wasn't familiar with the address. Regina had married and moved and I may have misunderstood when she gave me her new address over the phone. The poor taxi driver stopped at churches and knocked on doors to see if anyone knew where Regina's husband lived. He was a manager at a major department store and pretty well known even in a big city like Dublin. That's like going to NY and knocking on doors to find someone. We lucked out, a lady knew him. We arrived as they were getting up out of bed. Regina started notifying the family via their work and the police station and by evening the whole family knew we were home. Who needs cell phones!

We went into the city and of course the kids were in their element when they found a fast food place. Everybody ate to their hearts content. On the way home Regina asked what they wanted for supper. What do you mean supper, we just ate a big meal. They didn't consider fast food supper. We went to Carrickmacross and the yanks were a big hit, all the boys of the town were chasing them. One mother told me she used to have to beat her son to get him to take a bath, now he was taking one every day getting slicked up for the Yankees. All Americans were called Yankees. Young Michael was like the pied piper with all the girls chasing him. On our drive down to Wexford to see Irene Michael kept asking us to stop the car. He was fascinated by the mountains, he was a Floridian and had never seen mountains before.

Pope John Paul 11 had just been to Ireland so the kids stood on the hill in Dublin where he'd said mass. They had canvas sneakers and they got them all wet and muddy. Auntie Phyllis sent them down to the shoe store to get new ones. She told them to tell the shopkeeper to send up a few pair and their mom would pick what she wanted and send the rest back with the money. That was common practice at home, imagine doing that in America. We visited Gerard and the kids got to ride horses for the first time. Gerard put me on this fat horse with a saddle that was too loose. It kept slipping and I went with it until I was riding on the side of the horse. He started galloping towards the small side door of the barn, if Gerard hadn't grabbed him I could have lost my head. Somebody taped it and I was the laughing stock of the family. I have very bad luck with horses.

Welcome Back

I came back to America to a hurricane of a house, The kitchen sink overflowing with dirty dishes and clothes soaking in slimy water in the bathtub, shirts strewn everywhere. I was used to it, he didn't care, I was just the maid. Most of the time Charlie was MIA at the racetrack or gambling at the car dealership up the street. One time he won a car which I drove up to auntie Winnies with the kids. Our dog jumped out the window on the highway and we had to stop the traffic to catch him. One time Charlie won $3000 and told me to put it in the bank for safekeeping. I used it as my escape money and got Michael to move us to the apartments his brother managed down the shore. I couldn't work with three small children so I worried what would happen when the money ran out. Veronica took the opportunity to go home to Ireland on vacation with her twin boys and left her 2 girls and husband with me and once in a while the grandmother popped in. When my girls went to bed at night I sat looking at the four walls, I had no TV and nobody visited. I felt worse off than before so I called Michael and he came and brought us back home but nothing changed, Charlie wasn't even home the night I got back.

A Dark Time In My Life

I'm ashamed to say one time I was so desperate I contemplated suicide. I was going to ram myself and the three girls into a brick wall in our car. My only fear was that we might not all die together and I wouldn't be around to take care of whoever was left. Mary reminded me of another time I called her up crying and saying I was going to drown myself and my kids, that we'd be better off. She and her husband drove 120 miles an hour for 9 hours to stop me. I don't even remember that incident. I tell you this because your situation can sometimes be so desperate that you see no other way out except suicide. I don't believe I ever would have followed through with it but it scares me to think I even contemplated it. Beside I was Catholic and I knew I would have been condemned to hell, only God has the right to take lives. There was no point in confiding in auntie Winnie because she was from the old stock who preached "you made your bed now you have to lie in it".

Moving Again

We lived in Pemberton and worked in the stores for a few years but we never got rich from it, we had no experience and there was a lot of waste. It was impossible to raise 3 young kids and run a business. Charlie leased the luncheonette to a friend with the agreement she would pay us for the inventory. She stayed there a month, liquidated our inventory, then took off. No money! I was glad to be out of there. We later sold it and I don't know what happened if they knocked it down or not. I could care less. My only regret was that my mother's letters were stored away in the attic never to be seen again.

We moved to the shore taking over the townhouses his brother used to manage. A change of scenery always helped our marriage because it kept me preoccupied. Coleen started kindergarten. Her teacher told me she didn't like to sit on the floor because she didn't want to get her clothes dirty, she was a miss prissy. I did the renting of the townhouses and the leases and Veronica and I cleaned the townhouses while Charlie did the maintenance. We got $75 for cleaning a three bedroom and $50 for a two. One time we found a dead cat in a garbage bag. They were summer-winter rentals so we had students during the college year and Jersey city families during the summer. It worked out good for us even though I said if I ever get lung cancer it'll be from oven cleaner. Later Michael and his family moved down too. Charlie's mother and brother lived next door and Veronica wasn't far away. She was always having parties at her house, even ironing parties while she provided the booze and the food. It was worth it to her, she had 4 kids by now.

Some of Charlie's brothers were gamblers and the race track was close by. One time I was next door when their mother came home from walking to the supermarket, her arms loaded down with groceries, stepping over the boys while they watched TV. Not exactly the makings of good husbands, they were never asked to do anything. The mother had them spoiled rotten. I think she believed nobody could take care of her boys like her.

My kids hung sheets on the clothesline in the back yard and held concerts for all the neighborhood kids, Jen was the organizer. Even the parents came, a quarter to get in. The song "I'm not Lisa" was very popular then and Jen used to sing it, she also sang "I'm the happiest girl in the whole USA" sometimes while crying. One time she got up on the stage at a Fourth of July outing and sang "I'm not Lisa". She was only four years old. A lady at her grandmother's night club was bragging about her when her grandma said, that was my granddaughter.

Three Irish families rented a house for the summer and we all hung out together. One night we tried to smoke a joint one of them found in her son's pocket. We each took a puff, nobody liked it, I guess because we weren't smokers and we were so scared of getting caught, you'd think we were criminals. I thought Charlie would use it against me if I ever filed for divorce. I took a side job delivering bundles of newspapers to the delivery boys in Rumson. I was able to take the girls with me. I had it down pat, I'd leave the car running, drop off the bundles on their porch and run. One day a kid ran after me saying "ma'am, I can't deliver the papers today", why not? "because my house burned down". I'd just dropped off the papers on his porch and didn't notice the house had burned down, the porch was the only thing standing. Talk about tunnel vision. I put so much wear and tear on my car I don't know if the job paid off.

Every Mother's Nightmare

The kids played outside with the neighborhood kids in the cul-de-sac and one time when I called them in for lunch Michele was missing. We searched for her along the boardwalk and on the beach, then knocking on neighbor's doors, but couldn't find her. We called the police. She was found at the hospital where somebody had dropped her off. She was only three years old then, what a nightmare! We later found out a girl named Winnie had taken her for a walk on the beach and took her to an apartment where she tried to take her clothes off. Michele refused and she punched her in the face and bled her nose and then left her naked by the dumpster and threw her bloody clothes into the dumpster. Apparently one of the tenants found her and took her to the manager's office. He didn't want the police coming around so he took her in a grocery cart to the other end of town and knocked on a door and said he found her, the people took her to the hospital. We later found out that the manager was a drug dealer and that's why he didn't want the police coming around and Winnie was his 10 year old daughter who visited on weekends. I never talked about it to Michele because I hoped her being so young she would forget but it must have had a lasting effect on her because we later read about it in her journal. We got the whole story in bits and pieces, some she told us and the rest came from neighbors and the house where she was dropped off, the people were friends of her grandma although they didn't know who she was at the time. Another time she fell out of her stroller and had to get stitches in her head. That was in her journal also.

Auntie Winnie's Visits To The Shore

Auntie Winnie & Tom visited us on weekends, the kids loved having them. She'd arrive with garbage bags loaded down with books and toys which the girls used for playing school with the neighborhood kids. We had three bedrooms so each one had her own classroom and they'd stand and sing the pledge of allegiance through the heating vents. Most of the neighborhood kids were writing their names by the time they started kindergarten, thanks to the Jones "teachers". Auntie Winnie worked for Priests and they got all kinds of goodies donated by the bakery and she'd freeze some to take down to us. She'd take the girls for a walk on the boardwalk carrying a stick to keep them in line.

She saved up quarters and whenever she came down she'd line up the girls and hand them out. Afterwards I'd take them out to the store to spend the quarters. It never failed Jen always forgot her money and when she did remember she'd lose her wallet in the store. Finally she put a note in her wallet saying "this wallet belongs to name, address and phone#. If you find it please be honest and return it". Her keys were also in her wallet, talk about an invitation to robbery. Jen was a bit chubbier than Coleen and Michele so she made up her mind one Summer she was going to lose weight before she went back to school. She swam 100 laps every day in the pool and watched what she ate. One time we had chicken drumsticks for dinner and she asked what animal is this. I thought of the poor little chickens with their legs chopped off and I haven't eaten drumsticks since. Well, Jen lost 16lbs. that Summer, her teacher didn't even recognize her when she went back to school. Actually the doctor was concerned about the rapid weight loss. Tom and auntie Winnie came down the shore for years until he fell out with Charlie over not getting paid enough for cutting the grass, (we thought he was doing it for nothing) and they both stopped visiting. She made the excuse she was afraid of traveling but we knew it was because of him. He fell out with most of his own family back home. But he was auntie Winnie's friend and companion so we respected her loyalty to him and kept in touch by phone. We really missed her. The girls learned to ride their two wheel bicycles on the boardwalk. Actually we were teaching Jennifer, she finally mastered it and was going around in circles shouting look mom I can ride my bike when Michele jumped on her bike and said, if she can do it so can I, and so she did.

One Christmas Michele got a tape recorder and she hid it under the table while we were having breakfast. I was a screamer, always yelling at the girls to hurry up for school, wash their face, brush their teeth, get dressed whatever but when Michele played the tape back I sounded like a tramp. It really made me think, I didn't realize I was such a screamer. Lesson learned for now anyway.

Charlie Takes Off

By this time I was babysitting two little girls, it paid $80 a week which was a big help. Then one morning Charlie Jones packed his bags and left for Florida with my brother Michael. No explanation, no goodbye, no warning, nothing. I used to lock myself in the bathroom and cry wondering what was going to happen to us, how were we going to survive, what if I got sick who would take care of my girls. The owner of the townhomes came down to see me and said he was happy it was Charlie that left because he could always get another maintenance man. He offered me $80 a week to stay and said he planned on selling the buildings in the future and he would give me the one I was living in. So now I had $160 a week, all utilities paid, so much for becoming a millionaire in America but I was moving in the right direction and I was self sufficient.

Months later I heard from Charlie, he wanted me to cash in some stock and send him the money, he was buying a condo. I did as instructed in the hope that he was going to stay there. Then one day he arrived back. He wanted us to move to Florida and for the sake of the kids I went. I didn't want to be the cause of them growing up without a father, besides Florida sounded appealing and I thought he might have changed, no such luck.

Moving To Florida

The condo was very nice, 3 bedrooms/2 baths and around the corner from the elementary school. The girls started school, Michele entered kindergarten and I got a job with a Fortune 500 company which lasted 26 years. I worked nights, 3-12 hour shifts. It was hard working nights because I missed getting the girls off in the mornings, especially Michele who had just started school. Coleen had to grow up fast and be the mother. I got home at 9 a.m, the kids were already at school, I slept 'til they got home and spent the rest of the day with them. Eventually we got a dog Benji after a few other undesirable pets like the lizard Coleen kept in her desk drawer, or the Easter bunny who was litter trained but would never come to us. Their father said we couldn't have a dog so we hid him outside whenever he was home. One night a stranger came to our door, wrong condo, and Benji barked like crazy. After that we were allowed to keep him inside because he "saved" our lives.

The girls went to the roller skating rink with their friends every Friday night. Coleen babysat a kid and she'd take him to the rink and I'd watch him while they skated. The poor kid looked like ET and it was right around the time the movie came out. People would look into his stroller and you could just read their face, I made sure they knew we were just babysitting. Wonder how he turned out, the poor kid. Speaking of skating rinks, a legally blind neighbor invited us to go with her to the ice skating rink. I thought if she can do it so can we. It was the girls first time so I thought I'd better go out there with them in case they fell. Well, they took to it like a duck to water but not me. I was falling all over the place, I thought my butt would never recover. I managed to get half way around the rink holding onto the rail when the whistle blew and ordered everyone off the rink for half time. You gotta be kiddin me it took me 15 minutes to get that far how was I going to get the rest of the way. The rink was cleared in a couple of minutes except for this cripple half way round the rink. They ordered me off over the mic, like I wasn't embarrassed enough, they had to send someone to get me. I joined a bowling team with Veronica. It worked out good, they babysat our kids while we bowled. I was as helpless at that as I was at ice skating. Sports was not my thing, I had a huge big handicap and so our team won the tournament. Everyone was furious.

Charlie's friend moved to Florida with us, they worked together. One time Coleen came home all upset, he had unzipped his shorts in front of her and her friend. Strange how history repeats itself, thank God Coleen wasn't afraid to tell us. Charlie threw him out and that was the last we saw of him until he came down with aids and died. He got it from sharing needles shooting drugs. Michael and his family were living close by. We took young Michael to our house every weekend. He was into Michael Jackson with the gloves and patent leather shoes.

One Mother's Day the girls thought they'd surprise me by cooking dinner so they put me in a raft and pushed me out to the middle of the pool so I couldn't interfere. They'd look out the kitchen window every now and then to make sure I was still above water. I kept calling for them to come and get me but not 'til they were ready. It was a cute surprise but I was petrified of drowning. I was afraid of water period.

I was one of the few who could take a shower without getting their face wet.

Auntie Kitty and Irene came to Florida on vacation and we went to Disney. Coleen had just gotten her driver's license so she drove and scared the life out of us. Auntie Kitty was in the back seat reading oblivious to everything. We ate at an all you can eat restaurant and my aunt was amazed at the waste of food. If the kids didn't finish something she's finish it rather than waste it. I was sick that night and all I could see was her with a stack of plates in front of her that she'd polished off. She never wasted a crust of bread in her restaurant. The girls talked me into going on Space Mountain, they said it was nothing. I wanted to jump because I knew once you go up you have to come down and I was terrified. I could have killed them. I was scared to drive over a bridge for years until I did it on the back of a motorcycle and then I was cured. We went on the teacup ride and they were hosing down some seats where people threw up. That should have been a clue. Poor Jen kept screaming and I couldn't even comfort her, I was paralyzed with fear myself. Now she'd go on anything, the faster the better.

The Loss Of Mammy

Mammy and I wrote all the time, she told me she had to burn my letters whenever I went into detail about my pregnancies. God forbid you talk about that, did they think we still believed in the stork. When I heard she had cancer I felt I would notice when she was going downhill by her letters. They were always so articulate, the handwriting, grammar and spelling, one up for the nuns but I never saw any deterioration. The last letter I got she said she was cancer free but that was a lie, a cover up. I was pregnant again at that time. I gave birth to a preemie at 6 1/2 months. She was only 12 ozs. She didn't have a chance, she only survived a few hours. I'd had an IUD inserted and wasn't supposed to get pregnant. She was born with the IUD on her head. I called her Patricia after our Patricia. The doctor encouraged me to have my tubes tied, he said it was better to have 3 kids with a mother than 4 with no mother. I reluctantly agreed but I wanted to jump off the gurney on the way to the operating room for fear God would punish me by taking one of my other kids.

It was then that I got the dreaded call to say mammy was dying. It's the call nobody ever wants to get, we want our Mother to last forever. I went down to the ocean and started screaming and crying over the sound of the waves begging God to cure her.

Mary and I went home together, Michael couldn't get a flight out right away, he was in Texas. As God would have it, He let mammy hang on 'til Michael got home, her long lost son. That was the last time Michael went back home and the last time we were all together. On that last Sunday night the family sat by mammy's bedside and sang songs. We all kept up a brave face pretending she was going to get better and come back with us to America and she went right along. Her watch fell off in bed and she told me to get daddy to take some of the links off but save them for when she got better and put weight back on. She knew she was dying but she wanted to protect us. She was only 85lbs, frail and deathly looking, she was so tiny Tom carried her up the stairs in his arms. What a pitiful sight. She only lasted another week. Mary and I had nightmares that night, we were in shock at how she looked, I hadn't seen her in 2 years, Mary the year before. Daddy was in denial he told us we were all worrying for nothing, that she was going to get better and walk down the stairs. I told him to go talk to her and tell her he was sorry for the way he treated her. He went upstairs and came back crying. I asked Mammy if he said he was sorry and her answer was "it's too late".

My dream of ever going back home died with my mother's passing. I spent the next 20 years denying she was dead and as long as I didn't go back I didn't have to admit it. I wished I'd talked to her about dying, was she scared, was she ready, no one knew because we were all pretending. I later heard she'd confided in Tom and said "you know what's coming, you've just been through it with your granny Clarke". Thecla put on the bravest face of all, she nursed our mother to the end. She always called her Peggy and she'd say "come on now Peggy, time for your medicine". One day I was sitting by her bed when she lifted herself up and was looking towards a Legion of Mary picture on the wall. I thought the angels were coming to get her. She took her last breath the next evening as the church bells were ringing out the bells of the angelus. A big gust of wind blew the curtains open, it was like a hurricane, the heavens had opened up to greet her. She had finally gone to her reward in Heaven.

Tom dressed her in a bridesmaid's dress, Mary fixed her hair and did her makeup, she looked like a bride. No old brown shroud for our mother, she deserved the best. She always kept herself nice, hair done, makeup on so why should this be any different. Granny threw herself on top of mammy's dead body crying "God, why didn't you take me instead". Daddy was about to serve liquor in the room where she was waked but Tom stopped him. From the time we were young she told us she didn't want anyone drinking over her dead body and we were going to honor her last wishes. Drink was the curse of her life. Friends and family came by the house for the wake. She had a big funeral, all the businesses in town were closed even the factories because everyone was at her funeral.

As the funeral procession passed our house we noticed the light was on in her bedroom and the front door was open, it was like a sign. We knew we had turned off all the lights and closed the door. This was to be the first time music was ever played at a funeral in our church but we were so emotional we couldn't sing so the congregation joined in. I always dreaded the day we would bury our mother, I said I'd jump into her grave, I wouldn't let them throw dirt on top of her but somehow God gives you the strength to get through it. When I was young and heard the song "Danny boy" on the radio I often thought, one day that song will break my heart and now the time had come.

At the time of mammy's death several of my friends lost their mothers too. An Irish journalist on holidays from England started looking up her schoolmates from the convent she had attended only to find they had died of cancer at an early age, much like my mother. She started investigating their deaths and discovered some 30 years prior there had been a windscale fire at a nuclear plant off the northwest coast of England and the wind blew the poisonous gasses across the Irish Sea to the east coast of Ireland where most of the cancer victims resided. It seems most women of childbearing age were the victims and many of their babies born later in life had deformities. I was 7 years old at the time of the fire and there were days when we weren't allowed outside because of the grey smoke from chemicals in the air. My sister Regina was born a few years later with a big red birthmark on her thigh and has had a lot of health issues all her life. This journalist was about to release her findings when she was mysteriously killed in a car accident.

Mary was pregnant with her second child when mammy died. One time her heat was out during a winter storm and the house was freezing. When she checked on her newborn son he was sleeping in a nice cozy room. She got that smell that was present when mammy died. We know God let her come down to keep the baby warm. Now we knew she was in heaven. I felt like a lost child without a mother even though I was 27 with 3 kids of my own. We had such hopes for her, we wanted to take her out to America and have her spend the rest of her life visiting all of us. We figured daddy would go first because of how he abused himself but like mammy said, the devil takes care of his own.

Daddy mellowed over the years, I was happy to hear Regina and Gerard had a good relationship with him. I think Regina straightened them both out after mammy died. He and Gerard assumed she would cater to them like mammy did but no Sir, she was not catering to them. She told them they were going to have to pitch in and they did. Daddy even had her dinner ready when she came home from work and Gerard washed dishes for the first time in his life. Daddy eventually stopped drinking. What a shame mammy didn't get to enjoy the change in him, what a pity for all of us. Tom was dating a girl for years but wouldn't get married because he felt he needed to stay home to protect mammy. He married right after she died and later on moved in with daddy and took care of him until he died. Tom of all people, he took the poker to daddy one time when he was abusing mammy.

Home Without Mammy

I didn't go home for 8 years after mammy died. By that time Tom,Gerard and Regina had gotten married and started a family. I had never even met their spouses. I'd missed so much. Our house was exactly as mammy left it except Tom's wife was the lady of the house now instead of mammy. She was so good, she was just like one of us and made us feel so welcome. One night we decided to go to the Ballroom of Romance, a ballroom mostly frequented by seniors. The whole family came, even daddy. Gerard was there with his wife, they were years younger than most of the crowd. They had a raffle and one of the prizes was free tickets to the dance the following week. Gerard said with his luck he'd win. I think that was the one and only time he ever went there. A dancehall was the best place to meet up with all your friends. Remember, I grew up in the rock 'n roll era and most of them were still dancing.

Goodbye Daddy

Years later Daddy got Supra nuclear palsy, a form of Parkinson's disease and stayed in his room most of the time. I went home to see him and he told me not to sit on his bed, I might catch aids. He said he got it from second hand trousers Tom bought him. He didn't even know what aids was. I guess it was the lesser of all evils. He was paranoid, wouldn't let me open the curtains for fear the British soldiers would find him. He came with us to mammy's anniversary mass and as he was coming back from Holy Communion people were reaching across the aisles shaking hands with him, it had been so long since he'd been out. He was holding up the whole line. He lasted a few more years as a recluse, barely leaving his bedroom. Tom called me and said he only had a short time to live. I prayed he would live long enough to find peace with God because I always thought he had a very troubled spirit. One day Tom called and said the end was near that he was very peaceful and ready to go. That's all I wanted to hear, he had found his peace with God, it was ok to go.

Mary and I packed up and went home. Michael was in Peru and we didn't know how to get in touch with him. Daddy lasted about three hours after we got there. I had the opportunity to whisper the act of contrition in his ear. I always wanted to do that ever since the nuns told us if we ever came upon an accident and there was no priest we should do it. He was unconscious but the doctor said he could hear us. We went downstairs for a cup of tea when Thecla came and told us to get back upstairs the end was near. Once again, she nursed another parent. God knew what He was doing when He sent her off on that Dublin bus to be a nurse. It took daddy a little while to take his last breath. Gerard asked what was happening, I answered he's going through the tunnel, he said "there must be a traffic jam". Always the comedian!

I had peace when daddy died even though I used to think the gates of hell would open up and all his friends would be there to greet him. I changed the bed linen and slept in his bed that night with some of my siblings. When Mammy died we were scared to sleep in her room. Gerard ordered a horse drawn hearse, very appropriate for daddy and all the Gypsies from all over the country showed up for his funeral and camped on the church grounds. The police had to evict them after a week. Daddy went off in style. He got a big write up in the paper with a picture of his funeral procession.

And that was the end of mammy and daddy and their generation. Only two siblings remain in their family, one on each side out of 24. Now it's our turn to carry the torch for the next generation and I hope we raised them to be upstanding citizens, to respect others, do the right thing and not be afraid of hard work and above all make God the center of their lives. I never wanted to be a martyr like my mother. I often thought if she had stood up to daddy maybe her life could have been different but we'll never know. Most women were subservient in those days.

MOVING AGAIN

Back in America we moved to Boca Raton because they started bussing the kids to schools the other end of town to end segregation and it took Coleen an hour to get to school. We bought a foreclosure in Boca and the girls needed physicals to change schools. It was then that we learned Jen's pediatrician's suspicions were correct. They needed their health records for the school transfer and the doctor pointed out how she hadn't moved on the growth chart for a few years. I knew Michele had caught up with her in height but neither Charlie or I were very tall, I thought it was hereditary. I used to be relieved because I didn't have to buy her new school clothes every year. I didn't realize anything was wrong. I guess this is what the pediatrician had suspected when she was an infant. She went to Miami children's hospital for tests and it was confirmed. She would be short in stature and she'd never get a period and never be able to have children, something to do with the pituitary gland. And to think when my girls talked about what they wanted to be when they grew up, Coleen was the teacher, Michele a lawyer or a writer and Jen just wanted to be a mother and now that was never going to happen.

She started treatment with an endocrinologist, he asked her which she wanted first, to get taller or boobs. She chose boobs and so it was, she started treatment and ended up like Dolly Parton which later resulted in a breast reduction. She took hormone therapy for years. She eventually grew to 4 ft 9 1/2 ins. That 1/2 in. is very important. The doctor told us some kids didn't come to him until they were in their late teens, by then they were suffering from depression because they weren't developing like their peers but it was too late to do anything about it. Jen was only 12, the peak of a girls growth spurt. Thank God she was caught in time.

She'll be 50 this year and looks like a young 30. She had no other side effects from the disease, some kids are born with only one kidney, so it could have been a lot worse. Our new house had a swimming pool which neither of us had any experience maintaining. Charlie used to throw gallon jugs of chlorine in like it was going out of style. The girls came home one day saying some of the neighbor boys who'd been over swimming the day before were walking funny at the bus stop. I just hope none of them were impotent when they grew up.

Working For A Fortune 500 Company

I was working during the summer holidays so my kids had to stay home in Coleen's care because we couldn't afford to send them to the YMCA. This is when you really miss extended family, we never had a babysitter in our lives. They were discontinuing the 12 hour night shift at work and I didn't want to work 5 nights a week, three was hard enough. I was in a stupor most of the time, I think it's unnatural to stay up all night. I was on the lookout for a transfer opportunity when coming down the escalator at work I saw people working in cubicles and I thought that's where I want to work, it was customer service. I interviewed with the manager and he asked if I could write a letter, I laughed and said you don't go to school with nuns and not be able to write. He took my word and I got the job. There were times when I loved it and times when I wanted to quit but I stayed for the benefits and long term security. Today I'm enjoying my pension. Training took 6 weeks and you know how I feel about classroom training. Myself and another lady named Pat were the oldest in the class, I was 32. Whenever Pat asked a question the younger ones rolled their eyes. I was glad because I was too scared to ask after seeing their reaction. Pat and I became good friends for years. My girls loved her, she was the reason we moved to Boca Raton.

There were 33 of us in the class and when we graduated, I looked around the dept. of 400+ reps and thought I'm never going to get promoted with all these people ahead of me. My senior was much younger than I and that was a bit strange too, I was used to older bosses in my former working life. One girl hung a shingle on her cubicle every afternoon and we had marital counseling, she was a scream. Well, as luck would have it, I moved up the ranks not because I was brilliant or anything like that but mainly because I was conscientious and always looking for ways to make things better. Charlie used to say "the mentality must be very low if I could get promoted". Thank you for the vote of confidence, Charlie! It was a lifetime of hard work.

During those years Charlie wasn't happy about the changes in me, I was no longer the little subservient Irish wife he married, I was becoming more assertive mainly because of all the management training at work. They spent nine months preparing us for supervisory positions, teaching us how to handle conflicts etc. some of which went against the grain for me. I was used to telling it like it is, not this psychology B.S. but I had to follow the rules.

One Christmas Jen entered Michele in a raffle for a two wheel bicycle at Kmart. You just had to write a hard luck story. She won! Michele rode that bike up and down the street, she was so happy. Christmas was coming and I didn't have much money for presents, the girls were teenagers and gold necklaces were in. I gave them each $100 and told them to buy what they wanted at Kmart. Jen had me drive her all over town until she got the best deal on a necklace. Another time I washed their Barbie dolls clothes and fixed their hair and gave them back as new dolls. We had a chihuahua, Rambo, that used to jump all over the presents under the tree, we didn't realize he was putting his mark on them, all the presents stunk of pee. Whenever the girls and I had a disagreement they'd tell me they couldn't wait to turn 18 so they could leave home, déjà vu!

Jen in her gentle nature would console me saying "don't worry ma, I'll never leave you, not even when I get married". That's okay Jen! From the time they reached their teens I started fretting about them getting older and flying the coop, it was count down time. There was so much I needed to teach them, cooking, laundry, housekeeping, all that domestic stuff that mammy forgot to teach us. We can't stop the clock and soon they were ready to spread their wings and fly. Of course they're never really gone, they're always in your life, thank God.

My job was very demanding, if you wanted to succeed you had to sell your soul to the company and I did at the expense of my children. Coleen picked up the slack, thank God they were good kids, I always said one boy would have made a world of difference, they'd probably be killing one another. Michele and Coleen were honor students, whenever Jen had a project, we all had a project. She was smart but she just had to work harder, I never saw the other two study. I like to think they had their mother's brains, but I think they were just gifted. Jen won a spot at a music camp in Miami one summer. They put on a performance at the end of the season, some were dancing and I prayed "I hope they didn't give Jen a dancing part" because she had two left feet. They must have found out for themselves because they gave her a singing part. I was so proud of her. She took piano lessons for awhile but her instructor got a job as entertainment director on a cruise ship and that was the end of the piano lessons. She learned enough to play a few songs, she had a natural talent, I guess she took after the Clarkes for the music.

Michele was the dancer, she took ballet and watched "fame" and could dance as good as the best of them. Coleen was into cheerleading and guitar and competed at a festival in Miami. They were in ballet, cheerleading and music. Her cheerleading team won a trophy one year. They all had after school jobs, Coleen babysitting, then Sears, then a pizza place at the mall where the motto was, if you can lean you can clean. She sometimes brought pizza home. Jen worked at McDonalds, she didn't care about the money she was just happy to be grown up enough to work. Michele was in no hurry to get a job, she was Jen's best friend on payday.

Jen and Michele were inseparable, they did everything together. Michele's friends were Jen's friends. One time we had to drag kids from the bus stop to Jen's birthday party because she had no friends of her own. Jen wasn't very graceful either, one time she chipped a tooth playing basketball and another time she broke her arm roller skating. Like I said, we were musical not athletic. Coleen thought she was the boss of them all and God knows she had to grow up fast with her father MIA and me working long hours.

Charlie Becomes A Snow Bird

Charlie started taking off for NJ every May and returning whenever he felt like it, sometimes 6 months later. He must have thought he was a snowbird. He never sent any financial support, no communication whatsoever, too busy going to the racetrack and living with his mom where his food was cooked and his laundry done. There were 3 brothers living with her then, poor woman but that's the way she raised them. It was tough financially when he left because I had to carry the mortgage and a car payment and take care of the girl's needs. I worked all the overtime I could get but once I went into management there was no overtime pay. One time I went to an ATM and just prayed some money would pop out. I tried for $100, no luck, then $50 and out it came. I bought day old bread and veggies in damaged cans from the sales basket in the supermarket, thank God the girls had part time jobs that covered their lunch and pocket money. At one point I asked my boss if I could work through my summer vacation because I needed the money but it wasn't allowed.

One time Charlie stayed away for seven months. Coleen was learning to drive and on the day she passed her driving test we drove home to take the girls out to celebrate. As we turned into our street we saw her Dad's truck in the driveway, he was back, our hearts fell. Coleen turned to me and said "you do what you want but I wouldn't take him back". I had just gotten a mortgage rebate which would have made life a little easier. I had written to him and told him not to come back, I was tired of this on again off again marriage. I wasn't putting up with it any longer so I told him I wanted a divorce. I'd learned I could manage financially on my own, I'd been doing it every summer for years and we were all happier when he was gone. We had pizza every Friday night and a party with a bag of chips and soda on Saturday. Besides, the girls were older and able to help out. That night I saw him walking around the back yard and I felt sorry for him but I stuck to my guns, he had 20 years to straighten up, there was nothing left of the marriage for years. He moved to the west coast of Florida and stayed with his sister temporarily. Years later he came down with kidney disease and Coleen took care of him until he died. She was by his side when he took his last breath.

Michael lived nearby with his family. He had a pawn shop which he kept spotless and could account for every piece of inventory. He could handle money better than any banker and he could read and write like a pro. And he had street smarts. His motto was "if they don't pay you enough, you help yourself".

Lesson for my girls: Don't be so naive as to think a man loves you just because he wants to go to bed with you. And if you do, don't let it ruin the rest of your life, forgive yourself and move on, we all make mistakes. Don't put up with spousal abuse whether physical, verbal or mental. Don't stay in a marriage for the sake of your kids because most likely they're as miserable as you, give it your best but know when to call it quits. Don't lose your identity in anyone, be true to yourself. Don't let anyone belittle you because most likely it's their own insecurity that's threatened. The one good thing that came out of that marriage was my three precious girls. I saw a marine today with a saying on the back of his shirt that said "whatever doesn't hurt you only makes you stronger". How true!

NOTHING COULD BE FINER THAN TO BE IN CAROLINA

In the meantime my company was opening up an operating center in the Carolinas and was looking for volunteers for the start up. We'd get $2500 bonus and they moved us and sold our house for us. They showed us videos of a white Christmas and I was hooked. I hated the Florida summers and the constant hot weather and I wanted my children to experience the four seasons and an environment where people cared about one another just like I'd grown up in. We all went on a home search and left our two dogs with the vet. We loved the Carolinas, there were churches on every corner and the people were friendly and courteous, a rarity in Florida at that time. I knew this would be good for all of us, we needed a fresh start besides I could sell the house and split the profits with Charlie, we both needed the money. When we returned Rambo had been run over by a car when the vet took him for a walk. We were devastated, he and Benji were best friends. The vet got us another dog but he had no personality, not like Rambo. Coleen gave him away to an old couple who'd just put their dog down. My company put us up in an efficiency apartment until we found permanent housing. Coleen got a job with them and Jen and Michele started school. I'd heard negative things about the Florida school system but the girls were way ahead of the kids in their grade in the Carolinas.

There were 33 company transfers, plus spouses and family. We all stayed close and helped one another get settled and just about everyone stayed except for a few management people who used the opportunity to advance their career and then returned to Florida. I interviewed a lot of the transfers and picked the best of the best so we had a good team and soon got the operation functioning successfully. It was the coldest winter they'd experienced in the Carolinas in 35 years so our first shopping spree was to an outlet to buy P.J.s and warm clothes. I took half of everything in the house and left enough so Charlie had what he needed to live there until the house sold. He only stayed a short time and ended up letting Michael and his family move in. I was happy because when I went back to Florida on business it was nice to visit them and they kept the house nice.

Then one year I was filing my taxes when I found out the house was in foreclosure. I thought Michael was paying Charlie but instead he was supposed to pay the mortgage direct. I'd never have made an arrangement like that, I wouldn't let anyone mess up my credit. Michael swore he'd been paying the mortgage which was only $172 a month. I made him catch up but it went into foreclosure again the following year. I put the house up for sale. We also owned 72 acres in Canada which we bought on speculation from a friend. It was in the middle of nowhere and I couldn't afford to keep up the taxes so we sold that also.

Smart Women, Foolish Choices!

In the meantime I'd made another bad choice in men. You'd think I'd have learned by now. My friends would go into a hall and pick out the best looker or dancer and go after him, not me. I was happy just to have someone notice me, I was pitifully lacking in self-confidence. It was like "here's me, does anyone want me". I was at a singles dance one night when I met Devin and soon we started dating. I was an easy target. He was about the most eligible bachelor there but that doesn't say much for the competition. It was nice having someone notice me after a 20 year loveless marriage. Later I found out he was an alcoholic who was extremely insecure and jealous of my relationship with my girls. He wanted to be with me every day, never gave me a night alone with the girls. If I did get a night off he tormented me with phone calls keeping track of me. Coleen saw the signs and said "ma, I think if you ever try to get away from him it's not going to be easy" and she was right. We were involved in an apartment fire deliberately started by the tenants underneath us because they were being evicted. We all jumped from the second story window with minor injuries, thank God. Our two dogs hid under the bed in the commotion, we had to flip the mattress to get to them and throw them out the window. The flames were coming up to our windows and Jen was screaming "I'm not leaving without my Nike sneakers".

Devin, broke his ankles in the fall and I was stuck visiting him for the next year while he was recuperating because I felt responsible. He lived with his mom just up the road, another mamma's boy. He milked it as long as he could because he suspected I was going to take off as soon as he was better and that was my plan. When I tried to get away he stalked us, threatened us, told the landlord we were running a house of prostitution and called the school to say Michele didn't live in that school district anymore and as a tax payer he wanted her expelled. The principal called me and said he was going to ignore the call because she was in her senior year. How do I find them! My impression of the divorced men I met at this singles club was that they were pathetic, insecure, alcoholics, so bad that their wives left them for another man abandoning their kids. I couldn't imagine any mother leaving her kids for a man. I'd throw him out first.

By this time the house in Florida sold. Charlie was at the closing, I was in the Carolinas. I got $20k and he got $27k. I wasn't happy he tried to screw me out of $7k but a lawyer told me it would cost more to fight him. From what I understand he bought a Cadillac and a mobile home with his share and stayed on the west coast of Florida. Devin was giving us a hard time, he stalked us everywhere we went and there was no stalking law then. He had to hurt someone before the police could intervene, so we decided to move back to Florida. Coleen and Jen moved first and I was supposed to follow but I never did, I figured they'd come back. I finally got away from the psycho, he hooked up with another woman and when she tried to leave him he shot and killed her son who came to help her. He went to jail for murder. That could have been my

Coleen, they hated each other. She slept with a baseball bat by her side. One time he tried to run her off the road on her way home from work.

Lesson for my girls: Don't date a guy with an addiction whether it be drinking, drugs or gambling because they'll suck the life out of you, they are master manipulators. And don't think you can change them, they can only change themselves. You don't have to date the first man who notices you, know what you want in a man and don't settle for less. Watch out for a mamma's boy, you don't need an insecure child, you need a strong man. Enjoy your own company and that of family and friends, you don't always have to have a man in your life to make you happy. Learn to appreciate the little things in life and stand on your own two feet. You have to find peace within yourself before you can be happy with anyone else.

Empty Nest Syndrome

To my regret, Coleen didn't come back to the Carolinas. She never liked it there anyway, she was a beach girl and the Carolinians were too slow for her. She used to run rings around them in the supermarket while they politely stood back to let everyone pass. They could sit at a stop sign forever. She started dating a guy in Florida and got married after a few years. I wondered if she married because she was lonely just like I'd done many years before because her marriage didn't work out, although they're still good friends. I let her down, I was supposed to follow them but I changed my mind at the last minute. I had a transfer waiting for me but I didn't want to go back to Florida, I loved the four seasons in the Carolinas and the people were very friendly and genuine Christians. Life was more relaxed, not like the rat race in Florida. I missed my girls terribly, Coleen was my best friend. We used to go to the mall on Saturdays and eat lunch out. We were buddies just like my mother and I. History was repeating itself.

Later Jen and her boyfriend moved back to the Carolinas, and she got a job with my company, he got a job as a butcher at a supermarket. They just walked in one day and said "guess what, we got married". I was shocked but I'd known him and his family for years so I was ok with it. He was always willing to help but he was self-destructive, poor guy, he'd fix one thing and break another. One time he got up on the seat of my riding lawnmower to close the attic door in our garage. He fell off, broke the seat and went through our side garage door. They bought a house in the next town so we saw each other every weekend. Jen was a TV buff, still is. One Saturday morning I visited them and he was washing the floors while she watched TV. She never was a cook either. What did I do wrong? Maybe I thought they'd grow up and marry rich and have maids. No chance! Coleen and Michele could cook enough not to starve to death, Jen could live on McDonalds and Pizza. Good thing her husband likes to cook. She's good at everything else around the house and a loving wife, mother and grandmother. And she's every bosses dream employee, she works hard, minds her own business, cross trains in everyone else's job and jumps into their seat and does their work when they're out.

GOD'S GIFT TO US

Sometime later Jen asked me if I would help her adopt a baby. I knew she felt Michele's loss the most, they were inseparable. Michele had even told Jen she would be a surrogate mother for her. I told Jen to kneel down that night and tell God what she wanted, boy, girl, straight hair, curly hair. God knows the desires of our heart but He loves us to tell Him. I had just seen a Christian minister on TV and he said "do people think God is deaf. You only have to pray once in faith and believe that God will grant your request and from then on start thanking Him for what He's about to do". That's exactly what we did, we asked in faith and from then on we started thanking God for the baby He was going to send Jen. In the meantime Jen and her husband took foster parenting classes. One day Jen called and said she had a dream, she saw a little girl with dark curly hair and she felt that was the baby God was going to send her.

Jen called social services as soon as they got certified and said she wanted a baby in her house for Christmas. Three sisters had been taken into custody the night before, two of them had been fostered out, they asked if she'd like the baby of the three. The next day they handed her over to Jen at a restaurant along with a baby album. Jen called me and asked if I was sitting down because she was the youngest of three girls, the only brunette, the others were blonde and she had Michele and Coleen's birthday. Everything Michele had been in our family. How could anyone mistake that for the hand of God. When I pray I always ask God to let me know when He answers my prayer even if He has to hit me over the head. Well this was clear enough. Tiffany was here to stay, a little doll with dark curly hair. She was one year old. She was born the day we were celebrating Michele's last birthday and Jen got her on Alyx' birthday. At first Tiffy showed no expression because she'd been in 5 different homes her first year. She had a bald spot on the back of her head from lying in a crib. The mother just gave her to anyone that would take her. We were all there on her first night and when Jen put her down to sleep she lay on her back and spread out her arms wide like she was saying "home at last". After a year, the parent's rights were terminated and Jen and her husband adopted her. She was surrounded by two sets of grandparents, great grandparents and a loving mom and dad. God is good!

Lesson for my girls! Trust in God, He will meet all your needs. God tells us if we have faith as small as a mustard seed we can move mountains and this was positive proof. Pray in faith and believe God will grant you the desires of your heart and then start thanking him for what He is about to do for you.

Living On My Own

I bought a townhouse in High Point, the furniture capital of the world and moved there, just my dog Roscoe and I. My family was all grown up and out on their own. I'd never lived on my own before and I was so lonely. I went to bed at 7 pm and watched TV because I didn't know what else to do with myself. I had friends at work but they were work friends, they all had families to go home to. I met this little 73 year old lady called Bert at church, she was a widow and lived alone and we became best buddies. I visited her evenings and we did the thrift stores on weekends. She was so wise, just like a mother to me, I absolutely loved her. My only concern was that she was old and I might not have her around very long. I'm now her age. Bert died about 10 years later, she was a God send when I needed a friend. She was a seamstress and taught me many tricks of the trade, a good Christian lady, not too well educated but she could recite her bible from cover to cover. She really helped me on my Christian journey. We watched all the Christian channels together. She sewed my name on the inside of a patchwork quilt that she wanted me to have when she died. I never did get it but it's ok, I didn't really like it but I didn't want to hurt her feelings. I have the beautiful memories.

THE CON ARTIST

I worked on a technology project for 3 years where I traveled 3 weeks out of every month to Phoenix, Az. I was back in the Carolinas one time when I went out to eat alone. That was a first for me, I always thought of people who ate alone as miserable people with no friends. Well, I was standing in a cafeteria line when this guy struck up a conversation. He asked if he could join me for dinner and of course sorry me said yes. He must have seen sucker written all over my face because he turned out to be a con artist. He was an undertaker, an embalmer and I let him stay at my apartment while I was away to watch my dog Roscoe even though the dog growled at him all the time. He proposed after 3 months, he was older, more stable than those who preceded him but that was way too soon for me, I hardly knew him and it wasn't like I was miss America and he couldn't resist me. He borrowed money from me claiming his new boss was always traveling to NY to see his father who had a brain tumor and he was never there to sign his paychecks. Plus his savings was invested in CDs that wouldn't mature 'til December. I trusted him completely, he was good at what he did. I even gave him my banking information for when I was away. We went to church and Sunday school together.

I assumed most con artists were slick and handsome and you could spot one a mile away but this guy didn't fit the mold. When Coleen met him she said he gave new meaning to the word toad. He treated me like a princess. He said he'd like to visit me in Phoenix, when I asked for the itinerary he realized he had left the ticket in his shirt pocket that he had just turned into the cleaners. He went back and it couldn't be found. He accused the attendant of stealing it and the guy was fired. The owner replaced the ticket. I don't believe there was ever a ticket it was just another of his schemes. He took me out to a local Greek restaurant that he frequented on a regular basis and run up a tab. He must have conned them too because all of a sudden he wouldn't go back, he claimed they hired a new waitress and she wasn't very nice to him. I told him I had just sold the house in Florida so he suggested we buy a house together. He insisted he pay for the house, I should spend my money on my kids. What a nice guy! We met with a contractor who asked for a $4k retainer. Tony looked at me and said "honey, do you want me to cash in my CDs or do you want to put up the $4k, I'll give it back to you in December". Of course I put it up, no problem. I was back in Phoenix when the realtor called me saying she'd checked with the funeral home Tony claimed to be working at and they never heard of him. I called him, he said she must have called the wrong place, he'd call her and straighten things out. As luck would have it the contractor backed out of the deal and I got my deposit back, maybe he knew something I didn't. He did me a big favor.

Another time a coworker of his had a daughter he wanted to send to Washington DC on a school outing so he asked him for a loan 'til payday. He gave me this sob story about the guy being black and his daughter was the only black kid that couldn't afford to go. Well what do you know, he couldn't oblige because all of his money was tied up in CDs but he knew a sucker who could. He guaranteed me this was a decent guy and he'd give me the money back on payday. Well, do I need to mention the guy disappeared overnight, if he ever existed. Boy, was I a greenhorn. He didn't like any of my friends, not even Jen and her husband, he isolated me from everyone.

Whenever Coleen called my house he always answered the phone no matter the time of day, he was supposed to be working. She started to get suspicious, she had just watched a Sally Jesse Raphael episode on con artists and he met all the criteria. She called me in Phoenix, I checked with the funeral home he was supposed to work at they never heard of him. It was all lies. I confronted him and he had all kinds of excuses said he'd been meaning to talk to me. I threw him out and he had the nerve to call me next day to borrow $50 and he'd pay me back Friday when his CDs matured, yea right! My friend Bert never liked him, she was afraid he'd kill me and being an undertaker he could easily cremate me and nobody would ever know what happened. Coleen came up from Florida and she and her sisters went on a mission as Charlie's angels investigating him. They found out he'd been fired from his previous job and it was so serious they said he'd never work in a funeral home again. What could be so bad, did he screw a dead body or what! That was the end of him, another lesson learned at a heavy price, he got me for about $4k. He took my charm bracelet to a jeweler to be repaired, weeks went by and he never picked it up. I went there after he left and it was a pawn shop, my bracelet was history. He even wanted to trade cars with me, the girls found out his was a rental.

Lesson for my girls: I tell you this story so you won't be so gullible. Don't be so trusting of strangers. Don't let anyone separate you from friends or family because that's their way of controlling you. And if they start borrowing from you watch out. My advice, if they can't do more for you than you can do for yourself you don't need them.

Back To Work

At this time I traveled a lot for my company between NC, NY, Fl, Az and Canada. My career was going good. I had wonderful opportunities and God was right there beside me. It used to frustrate me as a rep to see improvement opportunities but nobody willing to put the effort into making it happen so when I got promoted into management I took advantage of every opportunity. I formed a broad network of contacts in technologies and was able to cut through the red tape to get things done. If there was an easier way to do something I found it and made it happen. I was referred to as the efficiency expert. I managed down rather than up, not the best strategy for your career but I believed if the reps had the tools they needed they would be happy and productive and we all benefited. I didn't believe in kissing butts although I saw it work for many of my peers. I focused on the people, I knew the management would take care of itself. I believed in treating my people fairly and worked right alongside them. As a result I had the highest producing team in the dept. which didn't always pay off because I got moved around to boost productivity in low performing teams. I only had to terminate one employee in all of my 26 years and she was already on step 3 counseling when I took over the team. She later thanked me because she went on to do something she loved. I took over another team and my first assignment was to terminate an employee that was always late. Sure enough he was late again on day one and had some story about his dog running away, I'm sure he used it before. I gave him the benefit of the doubt with a final warning. He turned out to be a great employee and later went into management. That's what I most enjoyed about the job, developing people.

I got involved in technology, specifically artificial intelligence (AI) which we hear a lot about today, also business requirements, training and implementation. It was very rewarding and earned me several monetary awards. One was a trip to Arizona where I received a $1000 gift for quality and productivity enhancements. When we launched these re-engineering projects phone reps were expected to maintain their quality and productivity stats without a learning curve. Moving from dumb terminals to smart computers was an easy transition for the younger reps because they grew up with technology but it was difficult for the tenured ones who were using a computer for the first time in their lives. They were afraid it would blow up in their face if they hit the wrong button. The training was not tailored for these people, it was one shoe fits all and whenever the development team missed a deadline they cut the training short. I took it upon myself to work with these people at their own pace until they felt comfortable. I was sent to Canada to do the same and they saw a 30% improvement in productivity within a few weeks. All it took was a little hand holding. I especially valued the tenured reps because they were the ones with the good work ethic and loyalty to the company, the young ones just came and went.

My three girls worked for my company while they were going to school but they realized it was not their cup of tea. Good for them! I admired the younger generation who kept moving until they found their niche.

I'm a big believer in the old saying, do what you love and the money will follow. My generation thought themselves lucky to have a job and the security of a 401k upon retirement. I took the Myers Briggs career assessment after 24 years and discovered I was in the wrong job all my life, that corporate work wasn't for me, I was a people's person. Imagine learning that 2 years before retirement, no point in changing now, right! Oh well, it paid off in the long run and I was happy most of the time and all my training was invaluable even in retirement. I have no regrets, I still have plenty of time to do what I love. I'm sitting in Florida enjoying my 401K today.

Mary And I Go Back Home

One time Mary and I went back to Ireland via London. The plan was to fly to London and then take a train to Wales to see Thecla and we'd all take the ferry over to Ireland. We landed in London and headed straight to the train station, Mary was loaded down with a Braille bible for auntie Minnie. Neither of us had ever been on a train in our lives, on a plane yes, but never a train. We went through the turnstile and stepped into the first car. I wondered why everybody was going all the way down to the end. It was very nice, I'd always imagined trains were shabby, all graffiti and stuff, not this one. We were very comfortable, we were the only ones in the car with a place to put our suitcases and a table to sit at. Half way to Wales the conductor came around, checked our tickets and said "that'll be another £15". I asked for what, because you're in first class. Then where is coach, follow me. We took our bags and followed him through several cars swaying and falling on top of people. I heard people say "I didn't hear the train stop, did you". We felt like stowaways and to top it off we had to go back for the rest of our bags.

It was always so refreshing to go back home. No more having to watch everything you said, no more political correctness, people weren't afraid to speak their minds even on television. It was like being free again. I could walk down our street even after being gone for years and meet people I went to school with, eventually it was the children of people I went to school with. I loved how people dropped in for a cup of tea and a chat, you couldn't be lonely over there. Word travelled fast in our town so people always knew when we were home and they'd stop in to say hello. We would join Tom in the choir and meet up with everyone after mass. It was so good to be home but now that I have a family here I would never move back. I never thought I'd say that.

FROM DARKNESS INTO LIGHT

I joined a Christian singles group, became a born again Christian and found a new friend in Christ. I was on a religious roller coaster, read my bible every day, was in church every time the doors opened and never watched anything but religious channels on TV. But there was a spiritual warfare going on inside me because I was too valuable for Satan to give up without a fight. I fell into a deep depression. Satan telling me I wasn't good enough for God and I felt He had turned His back on me. For three years I didn't sleep past 2am, I was sleep deprived and the job was very stressful. I was traveling a lot into different time zones so my sleep pattern was all messed up. I prayed and begged God to let me sleep but I felt He had deserted me, Satan was right, God had turned His back on me. He had given me too many chances and I failed Him every time. I didn't even feel worthy to look at His picture on the wall.

I went to a shrink, he explained we're all wired differently, I guess that's where the expression haywire comes from. He put me on medication, at first it was too strong, I was like a zombie crouched up in a corner on the floor. During this time I couldn't function at work, I couldn't hide it anymore so I went out on FMLA and stayed in Florida with Coleen because the shrink was afraid I might commit suicide. I knew I never would because of my religious beliefs but I might have done it subconsciously because I was riddled with guilt at letting my kids down and I couldn't eat or sleep. I was all they had to look up to, I was supposed to be their rock but I was just a pathetic broken down cripple afraid to answer the phone or go to the mail box in case it was bad news. I lost a lot of weight, I was down to 105lbs.

I wanted someone to commit me to an asylum where I wouldn't have to pretend anymore, I was tired of trying to hide it. I just wanted to be left alone, I didn't want to talk to anyone. I cried all the time and my mind was in total darkness. My self esteem was in the gutter. No matter how hard I tried I felt I didn't measure up. I felt less than, always trying to fit in, always having my guard up. I felt Americans were superior, they had the good fortune to be born in this country. I felt any success I had was just luck, I didn't deserve it. What if they found out I was just bluffing that I was a big phony. I felt I got through school that way, kissing up to the nuns so they'd like me. If I got an "A" I didn't deserve it.

Besides being a crippling chemical imbalance I think depression is a state of the devil constantly telling us we are useless, always reminding us of the bad things we've done, how unworthy we are of God's love. Never a positive thought, constant guilt. Much like discrimination, one is self inflicted and the other is socially inflicted. We tell ourselves or we're told we're less than, that we were born the wrong color, the wrong nationality, into the wrong neighborhood or social setting that we're inferior. We're our own worst enemy because we believe it and allow it to control our thoughts, our behavior, our success, our lives. What's the point we say, we're never going to measure up. We feed ourselves negative thoughts over and over again. God made all of us in His own image, black, white, red, yellow etc. He must have had a reason to add a sprinkle of color and when we get to Heaven we can ask Him what it was. He never intended for any race or color to be inferior. We know an Irishman (JFK) and a black man (Obama) who became president, the most powerful position in the world. If they could do it so can we, but first we must believe in ourselves. We must earn respect, it won't be handed to us.

It's All Up To Us

Just like everything else in life we can either choose to accept our lot or change it. But first we have to believe in ourselves, have the motivation, hold our heads high, stay focused, reprogram our minds, set goals for ourselves and believe that we're all equal in God's eyes. Nobody knows how we're feeling or what we're thinking except us. Negative thinking is what got us to this point and only positive thinking and hard work can get us out of it. I don't mean to minimize either problem, they're both serious and life threatening but we have to work on ourselves to change things. Nobody can do it for us, we have to do it for ourselves. I didn't mean to get on my bandwagon but I bet people don't know the Irish were the first white slaves at the hands of the British. We have many sad Irish ballads that remind us of it. If a man stole a loaf of bread to feed his family he was exiled to hard labor in a British penal colony in Australia, never to return. Families were separated and sent to the American colonies and the West Indies as slaves on slave ships many of them dying on the way and auctioned off as white slaves, especially pregnant women because they got two for the price of one. Irish were less valuable than the black and brown race so they were mated with them to bring about the Mulatto race.

That was then, this is now. Our ancestors may have had to come into this country on slave ships but now we fly into JFK with high hopes and the rest is up to us. We've got to believe we were all made in God's image and He doesn't make no junk. My husband used to say, it was a lucky day for me I saw the statue of liberty when I arrived with my suitcase and 2 pairs of knickers. A slight understatement, I had 14 pairs of high heels and a new sheepskin jacket. And yes, it was a lucky day I saw the Statue of Liberty and all the opportunities this country affords to anyone who wants to work hard.

A NEW LIFE

I always thought I was no good without a man, I needed one to validate me. I was successful at work, a boss, an innovator, a motivator, but outside of work I was hopeless, I was scared of being on my own. I'd never lived on my own, what if I got sick. I slept in a waterbed and I was afraid someone would break in and stab me and puncture the waterbed and I'd drown. I had a terrible fear of water. How stupid! I didn't know how to enjoy my own company. I always had to be around people. A night alone was a night wasted. Our Christian singles met every Sunday morning at a hotel for prayer and a buffet breakfast. After awhile I led the praise and worship. It was there I met Chuck. It wasn't love at first sight because he was a heavy smoker which I hated, a divorced man with a three year old child and I'd already raised my kids so I wasn't interested in raising another. Been there, done that! But God had other plans for us.

Chuck had been an air force pilot during the Vietnam war and was shot down, now he was in furniture sales. We started taking shag lessons with some friends, he was my partner and a great shagger, It's a beautiful beach dance but I think you have to be a Carolinian to master it, you only move from the waist down. I heard it was created by college kids who wanted to be able to dance while holding their beer without spilling it. I was used to dancing with my whole body like twisting and jiving. Chuck didn't need to take lessons, he was great at it but I think it was just an excuse to get together. We started dating and continued to date for the next 4 years, too long if you ask me but he didn't believe in rushing into things, he said you have to be friends before you can be lovers. That was a new one for me, I was used to jumping in head first. Finally he said the magic words "I love you" and he never stopped saying it after that. I'm not sure who proposed, I think I gave him an ultimatum, I was 50 years old at the time, I couldn't afford to be playing around at this stage of my life. Regina surprised me by coming out for the wedding and Mary was there too. Actually they thought I belonged to a cult, far from it, just a bunch of born again Christians who met every Sunday to pray. Drinking was out, my kind of people.

Chuck introduced me to camping and snow skiing. Having a touch of the gypsy in me I loved it, no TV, no phones, no way for anyone to get in touch with us. We started out sleeping in tents but after a few rain storms we graduated to a camper. Chuck was of Scottish descent and they're known to be very frugal. He'd make a list of groceries to take on a camping weekend. One hamburger, one hotdog, one egg each. God forbid we dropped something on the ground and the dog got to it first we'd have to go hungry. Needless to say I took over that task and I'd pack a dozen eggs, a pack of hot dogs etc, we had leftovers. I'd rather be safe than sorry. We walked trails, rode bikes, swam, barbecued etc. The only thing missing was music so I bought a guitar with the intention of learning to play so we could have sing songs around the camp fire but that never panned out, like all the other pipe dreams. His daughter loved camping and later my grandkids. Everybody looked out for each other's kids, it was such a safe environment. It's a certain kind of people that camp, I guess it helps if you have a bit of the gypsy in you.

Near Death Experience

One day I was leaving work and it was pouring out of the heavens. Some of the girls were waiting in the lobby for the rain to let up so they could get to their cars and pick up their kids from daycare. I figured one of us had to get wet so I went for my car and picked several of them up and brought them to their cars. I felt I'd done my good deed for the day and was heading home when my car hydroplaned and started bouncing down an embankment towards a ravine and trees. There was total darkness in my car, even though it was light outside and I saw a flicker of light in the distance, I prayed and asked God to save me and not let me die. My car turned just before it reached the trees and the passenger side of the car was smashed in. I kicked the driver door open and climbed back up the hill. People had stopped their cars thinking I was going to be killed. My car was totaled but thank God I didn't have a scratch. I now know what the darkness was and the flicker of light I'd seen, I was traveling through the tunnel and the light was at the end of the tunnel. It was a near death experience but I guess God wasn't done with me yet, He still had work for me to do.

MISSIONARY TRIP TO RUSSIA

I felt the call of God to go on a 10 day missionary trip to Russia with thirty one other parishioners, Chuck was very supportive, he said "if you feel the call of God to go then we'll make it happen". It was a very spiritual experience. We gave out bibles to the schools, as a matter of fact we reached the million mark. The school visits were pre-approved by the minister of education but at one of the schools we weren't being admitted because the principal was out. Would you believe the kids were pleading with the assistant principal to let us in, they said they wanted to hear about Jesus. Isn't that amazing, and you can't bring religion into the schools in America. There was political unrest while we were there and the police kept guard in the lobby of our hotel because it was known there were 32 Americans staying there. I had no fear, I felt like we were protected by a ring of fire and what better way to go than to die doing God's work.

We visited an orphanage where little kids were brought when they were sick but the parents never returned for them. They stood by the fence and every car that pulled up they cried mamma. They slept about 20 beds to a dorm, all the little beds back to back, it was like something out of a movie, poor little darlings! One of the couples in our team later adopted two siblings from that orphanage. Cars were abandoned on the side of the road because when they broke down people couldn't afford to have them fixed. People were picking food out of the garbage. My friends were shocked but they had never been outside of the Carolinas. You just have to go to NY and you'll see the same. Bathrooms were a luxury. Even in restaurants you squatted over a hole, no toilet paper, no sink. We carried a roll of toilet paper everywhere. We were excited when we found a fast food place in Moscow. A two story building, hamburgers never tasted so good, you just pointed to the picture on the board and they had real bathrooms with toilet paper. Children followed us all over town begging and wrapping their arms around our ankles. We saw the same kids begging all over Moscow and later learned the Russian mafia dropped them off all over the city. At the flea market the vendors were selling nesting dolls of Bill Clinton and all his women. It was during the Monica Lewinsky hearing, it was very embarrassing. I wish now I'd bought one.

Russian people were very subdued in public not like us loud Americans but they didn't mind pushing and shoving at airports and public places. I saw them grab a person in the theatre and throw them out of a seat because they wouldn't move over. We were freezing to death in our hotel room but they weren't allowed to turn the heat on until November. I noticed the young people were very attractive but they aged very fast, much like the Irish. The rough weather and hardships I guess. All government employees lived in apartments in the city and the poor people lived in the country. The government was on strike and govt. employees weren't getting paid, in some cases a whole family worked in the school system so the country people, the grandparents of the school children sent in fruit and vegetables to the teachers. You would never think anything was amiss because the teachers dressed for success and the classrooms had curtains and plants. The children were told this was their home away from home. The school children were very disciplined and polite, the teacher just had to give a signal and they stood up and sat down. Wouldn't that be nice in America?

I wondered if we wouldn't have been better served sending the money it cost to go there and just ship the bibles but we were told the government was so corrupt they would have kept the money. God knew what He was doing because years later those kids we ministered to were now missionaries to China. God just needed us to plant the seed then he made it grow. One teacher told me she wanted what I had, she said I had the love of God written all over my face, I was on a high doing God's work. I didn't understand why God called me to go, I was new to that church, I only knew the lady who had invited me but a month later I lost Michele and I thank God my faith was stronger and the people from the trip were there to support me. God is always planning ahead.

GOODBYE MICHELE, MY LOVE!

Michele dated a guy, Buddy, from a nice family but my concern was he'd spent time in a drug rehab. I didn't know it then but Buddy was still smoking pot and claimed it was no more dangerous than milk or alcohol. My Michele always seemed to hang out with the wrong people, that was one of the reasons I was happy to leave Florida, she had a girlfriend who was always getting into trouble. We argued a lot and with good reason, she was always up to something. She stayed out of my way, I guess she figured the less I knew the better. Later, she was very independent, had her own apartment, waitressed and went to college. I told her she needed to do better than waitress unless she planned on marrying the owner. She loved waitressing, she said every table was like a party, people were happy to be eating out together. That's one way of looking at it. She had lots of friends, sometimes the wrong kind, forever the popular girl.

Unlike her mother she loved school and told me she could picture herself a lifetime student, bite your tongue. She took off for the mountains alone on her days off, she really enjoyed her own company. She said she liked the peace and serenity of the creeks and mountains and loved to walk the trails. She liked to sing and dance and was very good at it although Jen overshadowed her in the music field, she was our karaoke kid. Michele stood back and let Jen take the spotlight. One time when we were out doing yard sales she told me you know Ma, you didn't do such a bad job of raising us alone, I said that's nice, what do you mean? Well, none of us ended up in jail. I laughed, that was her idea of a good job. She was looking forward to meeting someone nice and getting married. She said she'd rather live in a trailer and be happy than a mansion and be miserable. I guess she had a bit of her mother in her after all. Another time she had this English boyfriend, an only child who she claimed was useless because he didn't even know how to change the oil in his car. She could do all that stuff, she was very self-sufficient. I didn't realize she had a drinking and drug problem, I knew she drank an odd beer and smoked pot once in a while but she was always fine when we were together. She was good at hiding it but it was all documented in her journal.

She was making plans to move to NY to work for a publishing company where her friend had a job, she wanted to be a writer and she would have been good because she journaled everything. She told me all her friends met at her apartment on Sundays to discuss their problems like she was dear Abby. She said they didn't realize she had problems too, neither did we. She won employee of the month at work as did Coleen but she hated the job. She went to see a shrink once but didn't want to discuss it with me. I called the shrink and although she couldn't say very much because of HIPA law, she said she had a hard time getting Michele to open up. She also said she didn't think she would return but that she would send her some brochures. She was correct, she never returned.

Michele was killed in a car accident, we had just celebrated her 27th birthday. She'd been out drinking and went down a hill and ran into a telephone pole and it split her car in half. Her neck was broken, she died immediately. Had she lived she would have been a paraplegic. We never would have wanted that for her, she was too full of life. When I went to the morgue to identify her I prayed "God, don't let her have been mangled". When I touched her a peace came over me and God said "you don't have to worry about her anymore, she's safe with me now". If you have to lose a child what greater comfort is there than to know they're safe with God. At the funeral home a bus load of hippies arrived and then men in dress suits, black, white you name it, Michele didn't discriminate, she loved everybody. She reminded me of Thecla, a free spirit. They closed the restaurant during her funeral. The owner's mother always wanted her to marry her son but Michele thought Italian men were too possessive. One kid accepted Christ as his Lord and Savior at her funeral, one soul lost, one soul saved. I always worried about her, never knowing who she was with or what she was doing. Shortly before she died I put her in God's hands and asked Him to watch over her. She must have been too much for Him and He decided she'd be safer in Heaven where she couldn't get into trouble.

Michele, My Angel!

Months later I went snow skiing and I felt the sky open up and Michele say "so this is what my crazy mother does when I'm not around". She carried me up and down the slopes that day, I wasn't a bit nervous and never fell once. Any other time I'd fall head first so many times my mug shot would be all over the slopes. I regretted the times I went to yard sales and didn't call her, she was a gypsy like me, always looking for a bargain. I always thought that one day she might meet a guy and move to the other end of the country and then I'd regret not spending more time with her, never thinking she'd die. We fought a lot when she was in her teens but got along great when she was older. She was studying world religion in college and one time she was visiting she asked Chuck a lot of questions about it which he answered with great wisdom. I thought I need to write this down in case anyone asks me these questions. We said we'd continue the discussion next time she was over but there never was a next time. We also talked about death and she said she wanted to be cremated so that was an easy decision when the time came.

Jen was traveling for work and had to drive all the way back alone to her sister's funeral. She heard a song on the radio "In the arms of the angels" which was so appropriate for that moment. I always think of Michele when I hear that song. I prayed that some good would come of her death. I had a prayer "putting on the armor of God" which I found to be a real blessing and I felt God was prompting me to get it out to everybody. I added "in loving memory of Michele" to it, bought a laminator and made up hundreds of copies. Some friends took them on missionary trips and distributed them in South America and Russia. I put a message on the pole where Michele was killed and left the prayers there for people to take. All the years I had survived riding with a drunk father and a drunk boyfriend and here my child got killed by a drunk driver, herself. I was mad at her at first because she knew better than to drink and drive. Usually her boyfriend went out with her as the designated driver but that evening he was studying for an exam.

Lesson for my girls: Never drink and drive and don't do drugs. You can be happy without them. Choose your friends carefully because birds of a feather fly together. Get help if you have an addiction, it's a sickness that needs treatment, there's no shame in it, don't try to hide it. And for you mothers out there, put your children in God's hands and He will take care of them. He takes care of you doesn't He? Then why wouldn't you trust Him to take care of your kids.

The Loss Of Another Child

Life was good with Chuck, except for an odd confrontation with the ex. She brought out the worst in me. She hated me, said Irish people were dirty, they didn't shave their legs or arm pits. She made Chuck's life a living hell. The daughter stopped coming for visitation after about four years, she was only eight. Rather than go to court and force her Chuck prayed and felt God had told him to let her go for now, she would come back to him later. His heart was broken, what happened? We knew she loved her Dad, she couldn't wait to be with him and all of a sudden she didn't want to be with him anymore. Four years passed until he got a call one night to say she was in the hospital. She was air lifted to a trauma hospital in critical condition, she had endocarditis. Coleen came up from Florida, she was always around in a time of crisis. Chuck's precious daughter was dead within a week, she was only 12 years old. He felt God had let him down, He promised him she'd come back and now she was gone.

His heart was broken, he went into a depression. No camping, no vacations, we stopped doing all the things we did with her. He had a dream one night he was on this beautiful path, flowers on all sides when down came a little blonde girl on a white horse, she loved horses and was saving up to buy one. As they drew near the horse turned around and the little girl looked back and said "daddy, I love you". The dream was a big comfort to him, he was told she hated him, it was God's way of consoling him, and letting him know his daughter loved him just like God did with me when Michele died. He is our comforter and our strength.

The Birth Of Alyx

By this time Coleen had married again and had a daughter. She called her Alyx because she wanted a strong name, she pictured her being a lawyer, her father was a doctor and together they ran his medical practice. I spent every minute I could with them, I was there when Alyx was born. Her Pediatrician said she had Down syndrome but we refused to believe it. They said she had all the signs, a protruding tongue, the straight line across her palms, the distance between her eyes and ears. Even a second opinion agreed. They tried to do blood work to confirm it but her veins were too small so they said come back when she's 3 months old. By this time I was back in the Carolinas when finally she was old enough to have the test. I prayed and asked all my friends to pray and praise God the results came back negative, they even said she had a genius IQ. I looked in the mirror and thanked God and He smiled and said "I told you so" but I know the prayers didn't go to waste.

Every chance I got I was in Florida with them. I was lucky business took me there and I'd extend my stay. My first grandchild, as they say God's reward for not killing our kids when they were young. Alyx slept in her crib next to my bed. One time I was carrying her when I fell getting into their SUV. I tried to save her from the fall and broke my leg in two places. I went back home in a wheelchair. I used to have to take the cast off to get into my sports car. Alyx spent a lot of time with us in the Carolinas. Coleen had only met her Irish grandma twice before she died and she said she never wanted that to happen to Alyx. She was a ray of sunshine in our lives, she helped Charles recover from his daughter's death. In time he healed and we started camping again. He'd sit around the campfire telling Tiffy and Alyx ghost stories just like he did his daughter. We bought a boat and from then on we camped near lakes. One time we took the neighbor's boys and on the way home we stopped at a country store so one could use the bathroom. He came out all excited telling his brother "guess what, you can buy naked girls out of a machine for a quarter", condoms.

The Clarke Family Reunion

I lost track of Michael for a few years when one day I got a call from him out of the blue. Mary's daughter, Valerie was getting married and we were all getting together in NJ for her wedding and some of the family were coming over from Ireland. What a perfect time for him to get in touch. He met us in NJ and we had a great reunion, some of our siblings hadn't seen him in more than 20 years, since mammy died. Tiffy and Alyx were flower girls at the wedding.

THE LOSS OF CHUCK

By this time Chuck was starting to come back to himself. He made an Indian costume for Alyx for Halloween just like he'd done for his daughter and he loved the 2 grandkids. I'd pick up Tiffy on Fridays and she and Alyx would spend the weekend with us. One time Alyx was fussing in the back seat and I threatened I'd throw her out of the car if she didn't stop. Tiffy said "throw her out grandma and leave her there". Life was good but the fun all came to an end when Chuck was diagnosed with renal sarcoma. We didn't even know anything was wrong until we came back from camping one weekend and his back was hurting. We thought he strained it putting up the camper. After an MRI we found out he had renal sarcoma and it had spread to his bones. He was dead within six weeks and I thanked God for not letting him suffer long because he was in excruciating pain. My girls were there to support me. All his co-workers prayed with him whenever they visited him in hospital. I made up my mind when I retired I was going to volunteer at a hospital because I saw people dying alone with nobody to visit them. So sad and it was a perfect time to introduce them to the Lord and give them a peaceful death.

The ex-wife asked if she could visit Chuck on his death bed and I let her, I guess she needed to clear her conscience and I didn't want him to leave this world with hatred in his heart, he might not go to Heaven so I did it for him not her. She told him she was sorry and to go join their daughter in Heaven. He died that night. My heart was broken, he was the most gentle, God fearing person I'd ever met. He got up every morning at six and read his bible. We attended Sunday school together and he'd explain anything I didn't understand. He did his thesis on the Bible, I was a new Christian so he was way ahead of me in his Christian walk with the Lord. I was proud to be his wife, he was always a gentleman.

Everybody loved him. He taught me to be strong and have confidence in myself and I always said he tamed me, he didn't like to argue and I was born to fight. He made peace not war. Every morning he shouted upstairs at me before he left for work, "bye, honey, I love you". Thank God I'd been given twelve years with him, I just wish it could have been longer. He was my rock when Michele died, he arranged the whole funeral and comforted me when I cried. I used to tell him you don't know how it feels to lose a child, not knowing he was going to lose his own daughter within the year.

Coleen left Alyx with me after Chuck died. I told her pop pop was looking down at us and I'd hide little gifts around the house and pretend he sent them from Heaven. She was our little comforter after the death of Michele, his daughter and now Chuck. She wrote a note at school the day he died and it read "today is October 27th, the sun is shining outside but I'm sad because my pop pop is gone and he's not coming back". Her teacher wrote a note on the bottom "I'm sorry I know you loved your pop pop very much". He'd pick her up from school and she'd run to him shouting "pop pop". She brought the light back into his life after his daughter died. They even went out on dinner dates when I had to work late.

Did He Make It To Heaven?

Chuck was a born again Christian but not Catholic and I wanted God to show me he made it to Heaven because at one time I believed only Catholics went to Heaven. I'd lie in bed at night and stretch my arms for God to lift me up to Heaven to be with him, my children were grown with kids of their own, they could manage without me.

One night I had a dream I was in Heaven and Chuck was there. We danced an old time waltz. Now when he was on earth he could do every dance but an old time waltz, one, two, three, one two three, then someone would say hello and he'd lose his step and have to start counting all over again but this time he was doing it perfect. I thought, hmm! He must have learned in Heaven. We were so close I could smell his cologne, I could feel him breathing on me and then he was gone. I looked back and he was sitting by the water with a suit on. I thought isn't that just like him, what is he doing at a lake with a suit on, I had to teach him to dress down. He was in sales so he always wore a suit. Behind him was sand, then bushes with flowers. I thought how peaceful it looked.

Next morning the first thing that came to mind was how peaceful the scene had been in my dream. I wished I could draw that scene just so I could show it to people. I went to a department store that day and on the wall was a picture with the exact scene I had seen in my dream. I bought it and could point to the spot where Chuck was sitting. A movie came on that night "the five people you'll meet in Heaven" and low and behold they showed my scene again, this time in Heaven. I know I always ask God to be clear when He answers my prayers but this couldn't be any clearer. Chuck was in Heaven. Now I knew Michele, Chuck and his daughter would look out for each other in Heaven. I was at peace, I was able to move on. I returned to work for one day but my heart wasn't in it, my world had fallen apart, I was lost, so I retired. We were making plans to retire in January before he got sick. I wanted to die with Chuck. I couldn't stay in our house, there were too many memories so Alyx and I started making plans to go back to Florida. I felt bad leaving Jen but she told Coleen "I've had mom for the last few years you can have her now". I'm not sure exactly what she meant by that. I hope she didn't mean she was glad to get rid of me.

Lesson for my girls: Trust in God and He will send the right man into your life. Chuck enriched my life, he gave me confidence in myself which I lacked desperately. He taught me patience and trust and God was always at the center of our marriage. I'll never know why it was for such a short time but I'm grateful for the time God gave us. Treasure the good times because nothing lasts forever and when things are bad just remember they too shall pass. It's all part of the circle of life.

MOVING BACK TO FLORIDA

Before I left for Florida, Jen fell off a stage on New Year's Eve doing karaoke in a night club (the karaoke kid). I got a call from her husband at midnight that she was in the ER after breaking her hip. We stayed until she recovered. While I was sleeping over with the kids I noticed Tiffy waking up during the night looking all around like she was in a daze. We later found out she was having seizures. She went on meds for a year and was ok. It was sad leaving them but my plan was to come back every summer with Alyx and we did. A few years later Jen and her husband moved into our house. Jen got a job with the local college and her husband put a lot of money and hard work into the house. It was termite ridden, he had to replace the windows, deck and roof and he put in beautiful hard wood floors which I'd always wanted to do. They are very happy living there.

I was happy because Michele's ashes are buried in the backyard. I wanted to keep her close by so I could look out the window and talk to her. After a year I decided it was time to let Chuck's ashes go. I went to the lake where we often camped, the water was very calm and as soon as I let his ashes go a big wave came and carried them out to sea. I knew that was an act of God. Speaking of God; I had a bad day at work one time and Chuck wasn't home to cry on his shoulder so I sat down and wrote an email to God and poured my heart out. I typed out the whole episode and by the time I got to the end it didn't seem so bad after all. So I thought what am I going to do with this email so I typed "God" in the "To" field and hit "send". A message came back saying "God is unavailable right now". I had to laugh. He does have a sense of humor.

Back in Florida

We moved back to Florida and Coleen, Alyx and I lived together. A few years passed. Coleen got her nursing degree and had a real nice boyfriend who got killed flying his twin engine plane. One of the engines fell off, he could only be identified by a thumb print. She could have been with him that day, he was on his way to an air show which she'd gone to with him many times. She took it very hard, we all did, we loved him. As he was taking off that morning he posted a picture on Facebook of him heading into the sunrise, and that's what he did forever. There's no guarantees in life, we're here one day and gone the next so we always need to be prepared. Alyx and I rode our bikes back and forth to school with our little Pomeranian Puppy in the basket. We all got along great living together until Coleen had a collapsed mitral valve. It was touch and go. It took her about 6 months to recover, thank God she's ok today.

By this time Alyx had a little school friend who spent weekends with us and we all went to church on Sunday. They were best buddies and together with the neighborhood kids they had a party every Saturday night with pizza and movies on our neighbor's front lawn. She's all grown up now but we still keep in touch, she calls me her BFF. I met an Irish lady at church, Molly and we hit it off right away. Alyx thought she was a leprechaun she was so tiny. We started going to the Irish club on Friday nights, I didn't even know it existed. Molly had just lost her husband too and hadn't been there in awhile. She wasn't sure people would remember her, boy was she wrong. I might as well have walked in with a Hollywood celebrity, they were all so happy to see her.

The Meeting Of The Clan

This was my first contact with real Irish people in America since auntie Winnie who incidentally had gone back home years earlier because of ill health and passed away, poor auntie Winnie we all loved her. Everybody at the club was an immigrant from all over Ireland. No narrowbacks there. I thought I died and went to Heaven. They were dancing to the songs I grew up with and some new ones like the stack of barley and they danced like mammy and daddy, beautiful dancers. I met a retired Patrician brother who had been a high school principal in my home town. He said he only knew two of the Clarkes, Tom and Olive. I said I'm Olive even though I had long changed my name to Kathy. I met couples who'd been married for a lifetime and here was I with 2 marriages behind me, I felt like a fallen woman. Molly is now in independent living and we're still good friends. I've been blessed with some wonderful people God sent into my life.

I planned on devoting the rest of my life to my girls but after seeing all these happy Irish couples dancing and living life to the fullest I asked God if it was His will would He send a nice Irishman into my life. I trusted Him before and He didn't let me down with Chuck. I loved being among my own after 50+ years, I could let down my guard and be my old self. One time Alyx said "grandma, I don't like the way you're talking, you're talking different, maybe you should take speech lessons". I responded "I'll have you know I took elocution lessons when I was young". She answered "and how is that working out for you". She didn't like the strong Irish accent and the old slang that suddenly resurfaced, I wasn't the same grandma to her but I was myself for the first time in years and I loved it. The pressure of belonging was lifted.

God's Healing Touch

Years earlier during a bout of depression a shrink told me I should be in Hollywood, I was such a good actor. He said "will the real Kathy Jones please stand up". He was right, I was wearing a mask all these years trying to fit in, I was afraid people wouldn't like me for who I was. Gradually I was able to take the mask off and I don't think anyone even noticed the difference but I did. I no longer had to pretend, I was accepted for myself. I think this contributed to several bouts of depression over the years until God touched me at a revival in Atlanta, Ga. with old Bert. I was singing praise and worship songs when the spirit of God touched me, my blood boiled and I saw smoke come from my feet. I knew I was healed and I never had to worry about depression again because what God does He does for good. I went home and slept through the night, the first time in three years. After years of counseling I was finally accepting of myself and most of all I'd found the peace of God. I guess being told you're a useless good for nothing over and over again as a child didn't help build self esteem. I also had a very poor self image. I was only 5'2 with crooked teeth, big ears, varicose veins, bow legs and knock kneed. My father used to say you could hear me before you saw me with the knock knees. Some of these things I got taken care of over the years. Coleen used to say people like me shouldn't be allowed to have kids and pass on these abnormalities. I wonder if my sisters went through the same thing. I bet Thecla didn't because that one could talk to the queen of England. I always admired the cockiness of the British.

MEETING SEAN AND GOING BACK TO MY ROOTS

It must have been part of God's plan because He sent an Irishman into my life, Sean Kelly from Co. Tyrone, just north of Co. Monaghan. He was a very well respected person in the Irish community and had been active in Irish activities all his life. He went home every year to the All Ireland Final, he was there when Tyrone won, we have a photo of him holding the cup. He had lots of honorary plaques from the city of Yonkers for his role in the community. He was grand marshal of the Yonkers St. Patrick's day parade and worked on the committee for years. He too came to America at 18, worked with his uncle in the taxi business and started up his own taxi service, then bought a Myles Transmission franchise. He was a big brother and when the kid asked if his little brother could come along, no problem. He and his deceased wife, Sheila took in young pregnant girls until they had their babies when their families disowned them and they even sponsored young Irish kids during the troubles.

How could anyone not love such a good human being. We danced, we laughed, we cruised, we had house parties with our Irish friends, sing songs and storytelling, just like home. I fretted for a week when it was my turn to throw a party, remember cooking isn't my forte. Coleen used to say the smoke alarm went off every time I cooked. Sean and I shared stories about growing up in Ireland and we had so much in common we knew we were meant for each other. I remember vowing I'd never marry an Irishman but it looked like Americanized Irishmen were different. This Irishman's way of proposing was "do you think we could be happy doing this for the rest of our lives". Yes, we could and we are. The first time Sean met Alyx he said that kid must have broken the Guinness book of world records she talks a mile a minute. She looked it up and said no, you have to say eleven words per second to beat the record. Another time he told her to get something over yonder. She said "I don't know what over yonder means". This was a vocabulary she wasn't accustomed to. I was right at home with it.

That awful "C" word

I was diagnosed with noninvasive breast cancer which the doctor believed I got from taking hormone therapy so please, please try to deal with menopause without hormone treatment, try something natural. I had one lumpectomy and was awaiting another to be followed by chemo and radiation. This meant I'd lose all my hair and my big ears would be exposed to the world. Sean would question his judgement if he woke up next to me in bed with those donkey ears. Coleen and I went for a second opinion so I opted for a mastectomy via a tram flap which incidentally was the right decision because the cancer was much deeper than what they'd seen on the biopsy. I gave Sean the option to postpone the wedding or delay it for awhile because we didn't know what was in store but he refused saying he was in this for the long haul. What a guy! While I was recuperating he sent out the wedding invitations, booked the Priest, the church, the entertainment and the reception. He did it all himself. Tom surprised me by coming out from Ireland and singing at our wedding. We had a friend, an Irish Priest who married us and all our family and Irish friends were there. I thought I died and went to Heaven, I finally found my own people in America after 50+ years. We had both lost spouses we loved and felt their presence on the altar that day. We felt they interceded with God to put us together. We knew this marriage was made in Heaven, well that might be a slight exaggeration.

Life With Sean

Sean was the best nurse while I was recuperating he practically killed me with kindness. At times I wished he'd just leave me alone, close the bedroom door and let me sleep. Over the next few years we spent our winters in Florida and summers in his home called the Tyrone House in Block Island. Tiffy and Alyx came with us. Block Island is paradise, a little piece of Ireland. Sean has an upside down house with the kitchen and living room on the second floor so you have the benefit of sitting out on the deck and enjoying the green fields and the boats coming in. You have to take a plane or ferry to get there. Another place of escape just like camping. The only downfall is if you get sick you have to be flown off the Island to a nearby hospital which happened many times with Sean. Buddy our dog loved sneaking up on the deer which came right up to our door. One minute you saw him chasing the deer up the road, the next you saw the deer chasing him back home. There is life after retirement and the death of a spouse if you let God lead the way.

We've been back to Ireland a few times visiting both families. He's from a family of 9 also, they come out to America quite often. It's been 12 years now and we're like peas in a pod. Even the dog can tell what we're thinking. Sean has his own stories to tell like the time he confessed to the sin of gluttony in confession. The priest asked him if he ate 'til he threw up, he said no, the priest said then you're not a glutton. He is as awkward as a bull in a china shop, charges into everything, nothing graceful about him. I swear he was the case study for ADHD. Now that he's older and no longer hyper he's just ADD. When he was young the teacher was picking on a handicapped child and he jumped up and pushed the teacher up against the fire and ran out of the classroom and never went back. He got his GED in America. He regrets never confronting that teacher whenever he was home.

One time we took a trip to Memphis Tn. We were outside the Grand Ole Opry waiting for the doors to open and of course Sean couldn't stand still remember his ADHD so he started checking things out. He was way up front of the crowd when he turned around and shouted at me with a toothpick in his mouth "hey you, do you want to hook up". Well, everyone turned around to see who he was propositioning. I wanted to die. Later on our way out of the theatre a woman said "I see you two hooked up".

Another time we went home with Mary and her husband although we didn't sit together on the plane. Sean did as he always does, took the window seat, opened his belt buckle and got comfortable. But being the gentleman he is, he jumped up when he saw a short girl struggling to get her bags in the overhead compartment. You guessed it, when he reached up his pants fell to his ankles and he was in his tidy whites. Everyone burst out laughing. Later Mary asked me what all the commotion was about up front. Every time I looked at the girls across the aisle they were giggling. It didn't even phase him, he did his good deed for the day. Thank God they didn't have cell phones then or he would have gotten a million likes on social media. We were going home for Gerard's daughter's wedding. We all stayed at a castle that night and after breakfast Sean went to pay our bill. Gerard said when he saw the length of the register tape he thought Sean was paying for everybody, rich American right! Remember Gerard, the tight wad. Thecla, Regina and Mary came out to Florida on vacation. Sean surprised us by booking us on a cruise. It was the first time we'd been together in years. We stayed up half the night talking and reminiscing and it was the first cruise the girls had ever been on. So they were able to scratch it off their bucket list. The dining room waiter called us the Golden Girls. I think every woman deserves a cruise now and then. It's our vacation away from housework and cooking.

My Very Own Cleaning Lady.

One Christmas morning Sean turned to me in bed and said I didn't get you anything for Christmas because I didn't know what you wanted. I answered that's okay, you can hire me a cleaning lady. Done!

I asked my neighbor's cleaning lady if she was interested. She came in, gave me a price and we were all set for every other Tuesday of the month. On cleaning day I sat outside with a book and my iPhone and relaxed and thought " I've finally made it, this is my definition of making it in America, having your own cleaning lady, maybe next year I'll ask for a chef". A great smell of cleaning products filled the air and I was thanking God for my good fortune, no more cleaning, this is life. Finally after an hour the girl left and I inspected the house. She hadn't dusted, cleaned the bathrooms or nothing, just sprayed here and there to make it look like she'd cleaned. I was so disappointed so my plan was to fire her before her next appointment. I was dreading the ordeal but when I told her she said real brazenly back to me "I wasn't planning on going back anyway, I'm not a cleaning lady, I'm a CNA". Now she tells me! I'm still doing the cleaning myself, it's about the only exercise I get. It was nice while it lasted. I'll be smarter next time. Sean has slowed down and getting him up for mass on Sunday is a project. I call him 50 times and just when I'm ready to kill him he answers me "yes, love". Now how could you get mad at someone like that.

Serving God In Retirement

Sean and I were involved in several church ministries and volunteering at the hospital. Unfortunately he had to give it up because of his health. Corporate training could get you anywhere in life, they were so short staffed in the hyperbaric unit I sometimes worked 20-30 hours a week. A group of us go to the nursing home on Fridays and gather up all the Catholics in wheel chairs for the rosary and holy communion. They usually fall sleep half way through and we have to wake them up for communion. They're wide awake when we sing "God bless America" at the end. They're like family, all they want is hugs and kisses, God love them. I didn't get to become a nurse but this is way more rewarding. I consider nursing homes God's waiting rooms. I joined the bereavement ministry because they were such a blessing to me when Charles and Michele died. I especially enjoy doing Irish funerals because it puts the people at ease having one of their own helping them and I try my best to accommodate their wishes. They usually like the old familiar Irish hymns. I have the honor of being a lector at mass and pray every time I read that God will help me deliver His message. I even fill in as an alter server, that might be short lived now that I'm creaking at the knees. I always said when I retire I'm working for God and thank God He found me worthy.

I minister under the supervision of the most wonderful nun in the world who groomed me for my new journey with the Lord. So there are some good nuns after all. I'm honored to be in God's service. I've made so many friends through these ministries, now I know for sure I won't die in this country and have no one at my funeral. Our priests are the best, one of them joins us for breakfast. Why couldn't they have been like that when I was growing up. Actually, the nuns did a wonderful job of preparing us for the future, we just didn't realize it at the time. And that nice straight posture we have today is thanks to all the thumps they gave us between the shoulders when we slouched. In all fairness to them their training could take you anywhere in life.

PROUD TO BE IRISH

We have an Irish mass on St. Patrick's Day and the church is a sea of green, Irish hymns, Irish flag and a procession of the Officers of the Shamrock Club wearing their sashes from previous parades. I usually lector and it's emotional to look out at all these Irish people who like myself left Ireland broken hearted as a teenager to come to the land of opportunity and send money back to help out family. A lot ended up marrying Irish partners that they met at city center in NY. Auntie Winnie wouldn't let me go there, NY was too dangerous she said. These people sent their kids to catholic schools and Irish step dancing keeping the Irish culture alive. Mine didn't have that luxury, we didn't live among Irish people, I was the only Irish person working for my company. I was in charge of the St. Patrick's Day celebration and I set up a booth with some history, quizzes and prizes which they could easily get the answers to on Google. Myself and this Scottish guy in a kilt went around all the departments greeting everyone in Gaelic. Everyone thought he was the Irish one and I was his leprechaun with the pot of gold.

I always made the morning announcement in Gaelic at Alyx' school on St. Patrick's day and I'd go around all the classrooms teaching the kids a Gaelic phrase. I even filled in at an adult night school teaching Gaelic which they thought they needed in order to visit Ireland. You gotta be kiddin me, the only part of Ireland that speaks Gaelic is the Gaeltach although there's a big movement going on right now to revive the Irish language. There's very few nuns left and they were the experts in the Gaelic language. In Florida we have local parades and several St. Patrick's Day dinner dances with Irish bands. The young Irish dancers perform at them in their Celtic embroidered dresses just like mine. We're usually sick of corned beef and cabbage by the end of March. I'm so proud to be Irish, we made quite a contribution to America in spite of the reputation that preceded us. I think we've proven ourselves, we've left our footprint everywhere.

Where Are They Now

Alyx is now all grown up and in college. She works part time as a vet technician because her goal is to become a veterinarian. I see her every week and don't know what a day would be without a call from her. She's very proud of her Irish heritage and has applied for dual citizenship. It was she who prompted me to write this memoir and now she wants me to record it so she can capture the Irish accent. She wants us to go to Ireland before I'm too old (her words, not mine).

Tiffany is a Mom and her baby Sienna Rose was born on my birthday. She's the spitting image of her mother and a little doll. Jen is in her glory raising another baby. They visit us in Florida and we visit them whenever possible.

Coleen is a master scuba diver and an RN, she has her own home and shares it with her two rescue dogs, a pit bull, and a boxer. I have the honor of letting the mutts out when she's working on weekends, lucky me! We have a little rescue Pomeranian and Alyx has a chihuahua. I'm here in Boynton Beach tonight dog sitting 3 dogs because Jen and Sienna are visiting from the Carolinas and staying at Coleens, their toy chihuahua would have a heart attack with Coleen's big dogs, Alyx is camping at Ginny Springs. Like her mom she loves the water, she's a surfer.

Michael unfortunately died two years ago of lung cancer, he was only 62. He smoked from he was 12. My family came out to say their goodbyes, he hadn't been home in 40 years. His ashes rest next to mammy and daddy and little Patricia at home. He leaves behind three grown kids. Michael was anointed before he died but I still wasn't convinced he'd go straight to Heaven, I'd settle for purgatory. From the time of his death

I started seeing the number 11 every time I looked at a clock, Coleen said she saw it too and we felt it was Michael asking for prayers. I was convinced he made it to purgatory because the devil doesn't let you come back so I started praying for him every time I saw the number 11, it was like a reminder. This went on for a year and when Good Friday rolled around I remembered how God had granted me my wish many years ago. I went to confessions, made the Stations of the Cross, and prayed for God to take Michael to Heaven. I felt a great peace from then on and I hardly ever see the number 11 anymore. If I do, I pray for all the souls in purgatory. That was a close call for Michael because I felt if he can make it to Heaven the rest of us have nothing to worry about.

The rest of my siblings married and raised families of their own. We keep in close contact via "what's app". Regina is a widow living in Dublin. She has 3 sons and 1 grandson and is a special ed. teacher. Irene is a widow also, living in Wexford. She has 4 kids and 9 grandchildren, Thecla stayed in Wales, she's retired from nursing and goes home frequently. Gerard is married and lives in Louth with 2 kids and 5 grandkids, he claims he married too young, he ran out and got married as soon as he started going bald, claims he could have waited because he didn't lose any more hair, always the comedian. Tom is married and lives in the home place. He has 4 career kids, no wedding bells yet, unlike my generation they're in no hurry to get married. Mary lives in NJ, married an Irishman, has 2 kids and 4 grandkids who live close by. I have my 2 girls, 2 grandkids and 1 great-grandchild.

Sean and his late wife Sheila, the first NY Rose of Tralee and special ed. teacher were blessed with four kids, 2 boys and 2 girls. He has eight grandkids and we all get along beautifully. They live up north. He's 84 now and still maintains his gentle nature and sense of humor. He didn't know the meaning of the words slow down but now he doesn't have a choice. He's so polite my mother would have loved him and he thanks me for everything I do for him. He never lets a day go by without telling me he loves me and the feeling is mutual. Some mornings after mass I get back into bed and snuggle up behind him. That's one of the benefits of being retired. We live in Florida permanently now. Alyx and Coleen live nearby. I may not have become a millionaire but I'm rich in family and friends and the love of God, that's the real meaning of wealth. I never did buy that castle but who needs a drafty old castle anyway. I'm 74 and healthy thank God and hope to be around another while. I tell my girls when I get old I'm going to live with them and torture them like they did me and if I get bored I'm going to a swinging nursing home.

The State Of The Country

We're in the middle of civil unrest, riots and destruction everywhere. Rioters are tearing down historical statues trying to wipe out history and just this weekend they started defacing religious statues trying to wipe out religion. They want to take "In God we trust" off Government buildings and coins when this country was founded on Judeo Christian principles. The world has gone mad, the devil is running rampant. This is an election year so it's going to get uglier. I just put it in God's hands and pray that His will be done. I can't imagine anyone in their right mind voting for socialism, abortion, open borders, police defunding or elimination and the destruction of religion. They've taken prayer out of schools now they want to take it out of our country. I guess they're crying out for another Sodom and Gomorrah. God help our children and grandchildren. This is ludicrous, has everyone lost their mind. Covid-19 is plaguing the country, the world. I pray we find a cure soon and hope God will spare us and grant us many more happy, healthy years with our children. We wouldn't be where we are today if He hadn't carried us through the ups and downs of life so I'm sure He'll get us through this.

Life Is Good

I'm surrounded by some wonderful friends and neighbors and at this age we don't have to pretend, we tell it like it is. That's one of the benefits of aging, you lose your filter and people chalk it up to senility. I meet up with a group of women at daily mass, the priest calls us the Vatican girls and we have girl time over coffee afterwards, even the priest joins us. We tell him blessed art thou among women. We meet every Sunday for breakfast with six Irish couples. We have dancing at the Irish club every Friday night and the 25 card game three nights a week as well as house parties. I never learned to play cards so my girls and I have girl's night on card night. We order pizza and watch a movie. The Irish (snow birds) head for the Catskills for the Summer and the party continues up there. I swear God made Irish people to party.

My past time is bargain shopping, it's my therapy, I walk in and tell myself "I can afford anything I want here, designer labels without the designer prices, whatever I want". All preshrunk goods so what you see is what you get, no disappointments! It's a great pastime and it doesn't break the bank. Life is good, God is good! For now, most of these activities have been suspended because of the virus and so Sean and I sit in our den watching TV, admiring the sunset over the golf course and watching the squirrels chase each other up and down a tree and jumping in the car chasing after Buddy when he runs away. Exciting huh, see what you young people have to look forward to when you grow old. And I almost forgot listening to Irish music, baking Irish soda bread and scones and making shepherd's pie.

Lesson for my girls: We don't know how long God is going to give us on this earth, we're just souls passing through so make the most of every day. Follow the golden rule, be kind to people, treat them like you would like to be treated and enjoy the little things in life. Always keep God close to your heart because without Him we can do nothing. Pray every day for God to guide you and don't forget to thank Him every night for His blessings when you lay your head down on your pillow. Look out for God's presence in your life, He's everywhere, be still and listen to Him. We'll make mistakes along the way, we're only human but don't let them define you, learn from them and move on. We'd be pansies if everything went smooth in our life. It's the adversities that makes us stronger. As my friend always says we are where we're supposed to be. God doesn't expect perfection from us, just our best. Do things while you can because the day will come when you won't be able to. I hope that I have inspired you not to depend on others for your success, trust in yourself. You don't need a man or anyone to validate you. My darlings, I love you. I know I won't always be with you in person but I will always be with you in spirit.

Update: my girls thought they'd surprise us with another addition to our family. They got us a tiny runt of a dog for Father's Day, chihuahua and Yorkie mix. He's a little cutie but the last thing I needed was another dog. I tried multiple names to see which fit him best until the poor dog was as confused as myself so we settled on Bailey, it rhymes with baby which I call him most of the time. I should have called him Mikey because he can't walk past Buddy without teasing him just like Michael did with Gerard. Our good friend and neighbor passed away last night. I was there when he took his last breath but to my regret I didn't realize he was dying or I'd have prayed with him and believe it or not I'm seeing the number 11 again so I guess he's in purgatory and asking for prayers. Another dear friend died last week in Boston and Alyx got covid but she's over it and doing fine, thank God. It makes us realize how quickly things change and how precious life is.

Kathy Kelly

Some Monaghan Colloquialisms:

If someone has a wee want————they're crazy, their elevator doesn't go all the way to the top.

Mind yourself—— watch out, be careful.

Lay me light————move, you're blocking my light

Odd——————————different

Ach sure————but

Doting—————senile

Braces—————men's suspenders

Jelly——————jello

Jam——————jelly

Knock me up————wake me up

Footpath—————sidewalk

Gulpin—————glutton

Over yonder————over there

Vexed—————Angry

Won't ya have a wee drop a tea in your hand.

Sure and begorrah.

Isn't she a lovely wee gersha (girl)

Isn't he a lovely wee gasun (boy)

Get the babbie's dummy tit (pacifier)

Cheerio (bye)

She's an unmannerly scitter (brat)

If you fall and break your leg don't come running to me

Kathy Kelly

Some popular Gaelic Words:

Ceili——Irish get together

Slainte——cheers

Failte————-welcome

Slan leat————goodbye

Conas a ta tu——how are you

Ta me go Maith—---I'm well

Gora Maith Agat——thank you

Dia dhuit —————————Jesus be with you

Amadan———————————stupid, knucklehead

A Grandmother's Joy At Watching A Grandchild Grow Up.

Actually this book came about because Alyx bought me a tape recorder to record memories of her growing up. I thought it was my life story she wanted at first but she said I was around when she was growing up so she wanted me to tell her some of the things she said and did and if I wanted to do my story she'd buy me an extra tape. Very generous!

So here goes:

I was with your Mom when she went to the doctor for her last visit. She had preeclampsia so he told her to get over to the hospital right away. She drove, I was too nervous, I was a sucking on a lollipop out of each hand. I took the video of your birth and your Mom warned me not to take anything revealing. I swore I didn't but when we were showing it to friends she nearly killed me. I caught everything. You were born a cone head with a big red tongue sticking out. You looked awful to say the least. I had 3 kids and I never saw a cone head in my life. The nurse must have seen my shock because she put a cap on you right away. It flattened down overnight. Your mom wanted to call you Alyx with a "y" but I said that looks like a prescription. And I'm glad she kept it because it suits you. When you went to school your elementary principal met you in the hallway and asked your name. You said Alyx, he said Alexandra, you said no just Alyx. From then on he called you "just Alyx".

We did the stork and the flowers, you were the light of our life. We got a little scare at first but you'll have to read my book to find out all about it. Thank God you're healthy. Your mom had a french mastiff who slept by your crib and one day he put me up against the wall because you were crying in my arms, he thought I was hurting you. We played classical music when you slept because your mom had read it sharpens the brain. I think it worked. I stayed as long as I could because I was still working but I left you in aunt Judy's care because your mom was working. I knew she'd love you as much as I and she did, she loved you like a daughter just like she did your mom. She even took you and your dog Puppy to the Carolinas to see pop pop and I.

You took your first steps in a pair of white elephante sandals with the toes out and your nails polished. You took off in them like they were magic shoes but then you broke your leg on a slide and had to wear a pink cast for awhile. We thought that would set you back in your walking but those magic shoes did it again. One time you got a black Barbie with your happy meal and you said you wanted a blond one like you. We had a Pomeranian called big boy so you called yours puppy boy.

Whenever I visited you in Florida I slept in your top bunk bed. You'd call out gamma several times during the night and I'd answer you and you'd go right back to sleep. I worried what would happen after I left, there'd be no one there to answer you so I recorded a message into a talking picture frame and that worked for awhile but something happened and you lost the message. Your mom recorded the message pretending to be me but you knew right away "that's not my gamma". One morning I got up to use the bathroom but when I came back you were on the top bunk making my bed. I told you I was going back to bed and you said you can't I already made your bed. Your mom taught you to hang up your clothes and make your bed every morning and you still do it to this day.

Your mom let you stay with us when Michele died and you were a blessing. You went to daycare and one day you came home saying you had a week to learn your name, address and phone #. I thought the teachers taught kids that stuff, isn't that why we send them to school. I wrote it all on a sticky note and stuck it on the refrigerator. Every night at supper we would go over it. Sometimes you cheated and looked at it. When you finally learned it you called your mom and dad to tell them. We could see our reflection in the glass door of the preschool as we walked down the path and we'd hold hands and skip as we sang "We're off to see the wizard".

Sometimes you forgot to wash your hands when you went to the bathroom and I wouldn't let you touch anything until you did so whenever your friends came over you'd shout at them to wash their hands or send them back if you didn't hear the water running.

You loved McDonalds. My Donalds as you called it. You could see those golden arches from the highway. You'd shout My Donalds yea! I'd tell you My Donalds is junk so sometimes you'd say, MyDonalds junk, right gamma but when you really wanted it you'd say MyDonalds not junk gamma. Pop pop and I went to your preschool graduation. The girls chairs were pink and the boys blue. Yours was blue, I guess whoever set them up thought Alyx was a boy's name.

We used to make tapioca together, tabioca as you called it. Sometimes your mom would call me from Florida whenever the two of you were making it and you'd say "guess what I'm making gamma". I think you thought if we talked while you were making it it would turn out like mine. Another time we baked cupcakes during a snow storm and I sent you and your friend around to give them to the neighbors and you ended up taking money from them. Do you happen to know your uncle Gerard?

You started cheerleading and made lots of friends. You cheered at the games in Wake Forest and all the local schools. One time it was so cold and you all in cheerleading dresses I thought you'd freeze your little butts off. You were the flier probably because you were tiny and light. We even travelled to competitions. I lived my second motherhood through you. It was great feeling like a mom again. It's true what they say, you enjoy your grandchildren more than your own because you're at a different stage in life. You were the light of pop pop's eye also. One time he put you out in the backyard because you were fussing at dinner. He left you out until you stopped crying then he put you back at the table and you started talking to him like nothing happened and here I was thinking Oh God, she's going to hate him.

The family next door loaned us a crib and the mother used to say someday her son is going to say Alyx slept in my bed. We took you camping as a baby and one night you slipped through the sides and landed on the ground. I hadn't closed all the fasteners. OMG I thought you were dead. You woke up the whole campsite at 3am screaming. Whenever we sat at the kitchen table you'd say "gamma, what do you want to talk about", I'd say let's talk about the birds and the bees, you'd say "I no want to talk about the birds and the bees". You loved jewelry and you'd spread out all your necklaces on the table in front of you when you ate. I think that was the Jewish side of you. Your preschool teacher told me not to let you wear necklaces to school because the other kids might choke you trying to pull them off. One time I took you to an all you can eat restaurant and I think you sampled every dessert they had. Your tummy hurt on the way home and you said "gamma, don't let me ever eat like that again". You'd cover your babies with a tissue when you put them down to sleep, that was their blankie. Your favorite baby was Blah Blah. You'd push her in her stroller and when you got tired you'd throw her on the ground and get in the stroller.

We had date night at McDonalds on Fridays. I had just sprained my ankle and had it in a cast so I was moving around like an old grandma. You'd shout "watch me grandma" as you went up and down the slide. I felt like an old lady because all the other kids were calling their grandmas nana. When we got home I asked you if you'd like to call me nana and you said, I'll make a deal with you, I'll call you nana at home and grandma when we go out, how's that. One night you said "grandma, I was the only blonde kid there". That's right, not only were you the only blonde kid, you were the only white kid there. You memorized your first book and made it look like you were reading it.

You started kindergarten and of course I didn't want to miss out on anything so I volunteered to tutor kids that were having difficulty in each of your classes. They were mostly kids who hadn't had the opportunity to go to preschool or kids with non-English speaking parents. Fuzzy scarfs were the whole rage and I knit one for you and your little school friend. Your teacher liked it and bought the yarn for me to knit her one. You told her I loved candy so one day she was giving you all a clue how to recognize the word candy and she said "it's something Alyx' grandma loves". The kids all yelled candy. You loved school. Pop pop used to pick you up in the evenings and you'd go running to him. Sometimes the two of you went on dates if I had to work late. You'd pretend you were boyfriend and girlfriend. He made you an Indian costume for Halloween with all the Indian signs painted in fluorescent paint that glowed in the dark.

You had a crush on the boy next door and you'd spy on him out of your bedroom window. One time you left a note for the red headed boy across the street telling him you loved him. You were quite the boy chaser, weren't you, just like grandma. Whenever the neighborhood kids came knocking on our door to go out to play you'd tell them not 'til I finish my homework. You're the same today. School first, then play. When we went camping, pop pop would take us on trails and tell ghost stories by the camp fire. You had an overnight sleepover at church and you were up all night and you were sleeping standing up at cheerleading the next morning. We were all laughing at you, you practically fell over. You could put on that southern accent like the best of them, we used to be in stitches laughing at you.

One day when you were in Kindergarten you told me you had to learn your times tables by Friday. I said that's a lot for the teacher to cover in one week, you said "you have to teach me". Wow! I think we spent the whole of first grade learning them off by heart when I was at school and here we only have a week. We got a whiteboard and wrote them all out. You sat on your top bunk bed as I quizzed you every day and you were ready by Friday but I think you forgot them as quickly as you learned them and math is your least favorite subject today in college. I still remember my times tables to this day. Of course now you have calculators to do it for you. I was a bookkeeper in Ireland and we only had one adding machine in the office and the payroll clerk hogged it all the time. You kids today would die if you had to do all that math in your head. God forbid it might sharpen your brain. You don't even have to remember telephone numbers.... Siri to the rescue.

Your mom brought you on a Disney cruise and when you came back you hung a notice on your bedroom door saying "private, do not enter", I guess you saw a lot of those signs on the ship. You loved roller skating, ice skating and swimming. You competed in the east coast junior Olympics doing the butterfly, your favorite stroke. You took ice skating lessons with your little friend and could do spins. You were quite the little athlete not like your old grandma. I didn't learn to swim until I was 74, better late than never right! Now I don't want to put my head under water because it's colored. You used to tell the kids in the pool don't splash my grandma because her hair will turn green.

There was a scam one time where people were calling Grandmas pretending they were their kids asking them to send bail money because they were in prison. Well we came up with a password "we are the girls" if we ever got into trouble. We're still the girls. Remember when you and your friend painted my finger and toenails red and put lipstick on me while I was sleeping and I didn't feel a thing, then the two of you made breakfast with a menu and all. She wanted to be a chef and she's now in culinary school. You girls would dress up like models for church every Sunday. You wouldn't let her wear her boots to church.

One time you wanted to play softball and you made me buy you the whole outfit for tryouts thinking you'd get selected if you looked the part (your words). But it didn't work, they were looking for someone with experience. You joined girl scouts for a few years and made lots of little friends. One time you asked me if you could sell Girl Scout cookies in my neighborhood, you said "they're all old people and they have to spend their money before they die". Very comforting! We rode bikes to school with puppy in the basket, he was a big hit. When we first moved to Florida your first grade teacher asked if you'd ever been tested for the gifted program. You were average in the Carolinas but you made it into the gifted program in Florida. Go figure! Actually you didn't like it, you'd prefer to be in the regular class with your friends. One time when you were taking swimming lessons we passed a Jewish center with a pool. You said "I could go there Grandma, I'm half Jewish and half normal"

You're all grown up now with your own car and a nice boyfriend although we're having a little boyfriend problem at the moment. I say "we" because when you're unhappy I'm unhappy. Don't worry I sent him a text, everything will be okay although I don't profess to be "dear Abby" when it comes to relationships. Your plan is to go to vet school, maybe you need to get some experience with large animals back home with your uncle Gerard. Wouldn't that be nice but God forbid you fall in love with an Irish boy and stay there. Then who'd take care of me. Of course you already told me it's not your job to take care of me when I get old, it's your mothers. It's your job to take care of your mother but she got the better deal.

You're animal crazy just like your mom. The two of you would adopt all the rescue dogs if you had the room. I know any money I give you won't be squandered because you save every penny. You have more money than God, one of these days I might hit you up for a loan when I need an electric scooter. I know you don't mind spending my money, you're probably thinking I have to spend it before I die right!. I figure it's an investment in my future, one day I might want to live with you when I'm old and decrepit. You'd probably put me in charge of cleaning up after the animals. You're a good surfer, skater, swimmer and an honor student and the sweetest, most kindhearted person I know. I'm so proud of you when I see you run to assist people in need and congratulate military people for their service. You're everything I would want you to be. I'm very proud of you! When you open up your own veterinary clinic I'm coming to work for you if I still have my marbles and I love what you said that if people can't afford treatment for their pets they'll only have to pay what they can afford. That's my girl!

To be continued.....

FAMILY GALLERY

ABOUT THE AUTHOR

I was born in Ireland, number 2 in a family of nine. Grew up in a Catholic household surrounded by my Mother's family. We were into music especially singing in concerts and the church choir. I came to America at 18 to get rich and then I was returning home. My intent was never to stay for good, I loved my family too much. I'm still here after 56 years although my interpretation of wealth has changed dramatically, it's not all about money. My mother died at 49 so my dreams of going back home got crushed besides I got married and raised a family and now my home is with my children. I was very naïve when I came to America, I took everything at face value but after a few bad experiences I woke up to the ways of the world. It was all or nothing with me so I was very competitive at work, I always had to prove myself. After a few bouts of depression I found peace with God and myself. I lost a daughter and a husband but with the grace of God I was able to move on. I'm now retired and living in Florida enjoying the rewards of my hard earned 401k and social security.

This is my first book and I wrote it for my children and grandchildren. I've had editorials printed in the Irish Voice expressing my opinion about political issues.

Printed in the United States
By Bookmasters